Social Issues
in Literature

Women's Issues in Zora Neale Hurston's *Their Eyes Were Watching God*

Other Books in the Social Issues in Literature Series:

Social Issues
in Literature

Women's Issues in Zora Neale Hurston's *Their Eyes Were Watching God*

Gary Wiener, Book Editor

GREENHAVEN PRESS
A part of Gale, Cengage Learning

GALE
CENGAGE Learning®

Detroit • New York • San Francisco • New Haven, Conn • Waterville, Maine • London

Elizabeth Des Chenes, *Managing Editor*

© 2012 Greenhaven Press, a part of Gale, Cengage Learning

Gale and Greenhaven Press are registered trademarks used herein under license.

For more information, contact:
Greenhaven Press
27500 Drake Rd.
Farmington Hills, MI 48331-3535
Or you can visit our Internet site at gale.cengage.com

For product information and technology assistance, contact us at

Gale Customer Support, 1-800-877-4253
For permission to use material from this text or product, submit all requests online at
www.cengage.com/permissions

Further permissions questions can be emailed to permissionrequest@cengage.com

Articles in Greenhaven Press anthologies are often edited for length to meet page require-ments. In addition, original titles of these works are changed to clearly present the main thesis and to explicitly indicate the author's opinion. Every effort is made to ensure that Greenhaven Press accurately reflects the original intent of the authors. Every effort has been made to trace the owners of copyrighted material.

Cover photograph copyright © Everett Collection Inc./Alamy

LIBRARY OF CONGRESS CATALOGING-IN-PUBLICATION DATA

Women's issues in Zora Neale Hurston's Their eyes were watching God / Gary Wiener, book editor.
    p. cm. -- (Social issues in literature)
  Includes bibliographical references and index.
  ISBN 978-0-7377-5821-4 (hardcover) -- ISBN 978-0-7377-5822-1 (pbk.)
  1. Hurston, Zora Neale. Their eyes were watching God. 2. Hurston, Zora Neale--Political and social views. 3. African American women in literature. 4. Women in literature. I. Wiener, Gary.
  PS3515.U789T639 2012
  813'.52--dc23
                                         2011051843

Printed in Mexico
2 3 4 5 6 7 16 15 14 13 12

Contents

Janie Crawford's daring quest to find happiness and break free from the constraints of the traditional roles society demands for women is a model for those of all races.

Their Eyes Were Watching God is both a bildungsroman, or novel of education, and a romance. But in order for Janie to arrive at the full self-understanding necessary for a bildungsroman, Hurston must reject the other half of her story, the romance.

Their Eyes Were Watching God is the story of an ironic and failed quest in which the protagonist, Janie Crawford, will eventually die of rabies.

Chapter 3: Contemporary Perspectives on Women's Issues

Women should not try to gain equality by emulating men because women and men are different. They should instead establish their own models of the heroic female.

Rates of domestic violence and murder among African Americans are disproportionately high, and not just in poverty-stricken areas. There are a number of social factors that play into these statistics.

African American women who are victims of discrimination and harassment in the workplace find it difficult to garner sympathy, right the wrong, and gain closure.

Typical stereotypes, including the mammy, matriarch, breeder, and Jezebel, enable the dominant society to cast black women as problematic and so to exercise control over them.

Introduction

Zora Neale Hurston's modern classic *Their Eyes Were Watching God* has been so successful, so universally taught in high schools and college campuses, that it might surprise the twenty-first century reader to know that in the 1960s the book was out of print and its author buried in an unmarked pauper's grave. It took novelist Alice Walker's odyssey to the Garden of Heavenly Rest cemetery in Fort Pierce, Florida, and her subsequent *Ms.* magazine article "In Search of Zora Neale Hurston," to resurrect the author and her work. Walker called *Their Eyes Were Watching God* "as necessary to me and to other women as air and water,"[1] and bemoaned the fact that in the mid-1970s, almost no one had heard of it. Today, of course, Hurston's fictional biography of Janie Mae Crawford Killicks Starks Woods has been fully resurrected and restored to prominence as a great American novel by over thirty years of scholarship. As novelist Zadie Smith puts it, "[Hurston] has gone from being a well-kept, well-loved secret among black women of my mother's generation to [being] an entire literary industry."[2] Hurston is seen as the godmother, the kindred spirit of all subsequent African American women writers from Toni Morrison to Gloria Naylor to Walker herself.

From the opening words of *Their Eyes Were Watching God*, readers sense that they are listening to a master storyteller. Amazingly, Hurston penned *Their Eyes Were Watching God* during a seven-week stretch while living in Haiti. Given the necessities that came with being an African American woman writer in the 1930s, Hurston had to fashion the novel's beginning in such a way that it would attract a reading audience that was overwhelmingly white. As an example of just how difficult it was for an African American writer to gain the support of the arts community, consider that *A Raisin in the Sun*, the first all–African American play on Broadway, was not produced until 1959, less than a year before Hurston's death. Hurston's own play, *Mule Bone*, cowritten with the acclaimed Harlem Renaissance poet Langston Hughes, finally found an audience in 1991.

Hurston had begun her first novel, *Jonah's Gourd Vine*, published in 1934, with the vernacular voice: "God was grumbling his thunder and playing the zig zag lightning thru his fingers." Although *Jonah's Gourd Vine* garnered some positive reviews, it was a minor blip on the literary scene. Perhaps Hurston knew that *Their Eyes Were Watching God* would go beyond *Jonah's Gourd Vine*, which was roughly her own family's biography, the family history of her father's and mother's marriage. In *Their Eyes Were Watching God*, Hurston attempts to write an important novel, a novel that will rank with those of other modernist masters of American fiction. And an important novel demands a grandiose opening, a majestic statement about the nature of being, society, individualism, or happiness. Thus,

> All happy families are alike; each unhappy family is unhappy in its own way.
>
> —*Leo Tolstoy,* Anna Karenina

> It is a truth universally acknowledged, that a single man in possession of a good fortune, must be in want of a wife.
>
> —*Jane Austen,* Pride and Prejudice

> It was the best of times, it was the worst of times, it was the age of wisdom, it was the age of foolishness.
>
> —*Charles Dickens,* A Tale of Two Cities

Janie Crawford's story actually begins with these lines in Chapter 2:

> "I know exactly what Ah got to tell yuh, but it's hard to know where to start at."

> "Ah ain't never seen mah papa. And Ah didn't know 'im if Ah did. Mah mama neither."

But Hurston could never have begun her novel this way and garnered the greater acceptance that she was seeking. Instead she opts for the grand, sweeping opening, in the tradition of Tolstoy, Austen, and Dickens:

> Ships at a distance have every man's wish on board.

Given that this is to be a novel about a woman, and a poor Southern black woman at that, Hurston begins oddly: "Ships at a distance have every *man's* wish on board," she writes, not every *woman's*. Her choice of gender derives from necessity. For Hurston to gain acceptance in the fraternity that is the Great American novel, she had to prove that she could run with the masters: Nathaniel Hawthorne, Herman Melville, Mark Twain, Ernest Hemingway, F. Scott Fitzgerald, John Dos Passos, Theodore Dreiser, and others. Her novel begins by speaking of men.

Hurston seems to be using the form of "man" that is now considered sexist, the same "man" that we find in "mankind" or "man-made," the designation that by default applies to both men and women:

> Ships at a distance have every man's wish on board. For some they come in with the tide. For others they sail forever on the horizon, never out of sight, never landing until the Watcher turns his eyes away in resignation, his dreams mocked to death by Time. That is the life of men.

But, as we see two words later, she really is referring only to the life of *men*. The concluding sentence, "That is the life of men," simple, direct and powerful, is followed by a dramatic change of direction at the beginning of paragraph two: "Now, women . . ." With these two words, Hurston signals to the reader that her focus is to be on women's issues. It is a challenge, a dare, an in-your-face maneuver. Men have been summed up and dismissed in paragraph one. But for women, hope has a completely different definition. It is not exactly Emily Dickinson's "'Hope' is the thing with feathers . . ." but it is not far off. For Hurston's women, as for Dickinson, hope "sings the tune without the words and never stops at all." As Hurston suggests, the hopes of poor, black, orphaned, southern women rarely come to fruition. Therefore, "The Dream is the Truth." Years later, Hurston's erstwhile collaborator Langston Hughes would ask, "What happens to a dream deferred?"[3] Zora Neale Hurston already knew the answer. Women cannot hope to achieve their goals in a male-dominated culture and world, she suggests. They must act accordingly.

In the third paragraph, Hurston begins to show exactly how one particular woman will go about acting accordingly. With the first sentence, Hurston completes her shift in focus from all of humankind to women to one particular woman: "Now the beginning of this was a woman. . . ." The biblical echo is unmistakable: "In the beginning God created the heavens and the earth" (Genesis 1:1). But Hurston is not writing a man's bible here. She is writing a woman's manifesto. Or, as the poet Sharon Olds once called it, a "Womanifesto."

In 1983 Alice Walker, in her collection of essays *In Search of Our Mothers' Gardens: Womanist Prose*, coined the term "womanist" as a synonym for black feminism. Here, in part, is Walker's definition of "womanist":

1. From *womanish*. (Opp. of "girlish," i.e., frivolous, irresponsible, not serious.) A black feminist or feminist of color. From the black folk expression of mothers to female children, "You acting womanish," i.e., like a woman. Usually referring to outrageous, audacious, courageous or *willful* behavior. Wanting to know more and in greater depth than is considered "good" for one.

Their Eyes Were Watching God is a fictional dramatization of Walker's concept. With the deliberate echo of the book of Genesis in paragraph three, Hurston sets out to construct her own bible, not the white man's or even the white person's bible, but a bible for African American women. One only needs to consider the pear tree of Chapter 2 or the flood of

Chapter 19 to see Hurston working out this motif. The novel's third paragraph is a biblical microcosm in itself: Hurston considers Genesis to Revelation, alpha to omega, in the first and last sentence: "So the beginning . . . their eyes flung wide open in judgment."

The motif of all of creation from the beginning to the end is picked up in the last line of the poetic first paragraph of Chapter 2 as well: "Dawn and doom was in the branches."

All of this adds up to a daring assertion. Hurston depicts Janie Crawford's universal qualities and appeal—she is everyone. To suggest in 1937, that a poor, southern, orphaned African American woman is "everyman" was a radical notion. But that is Hurston's point. Janie is all of humanity, and even has a sizable portion of the everlasting in her: witness her initials, J.C., suggestive of Jesus Christ, or the nickname she was given as a child: "De useter call me alphabet." Alphabet encompasses all possibilities. For a writer, as Kurt Vonnegut notes in his book *A Man Without a Country*, possibility includes "twenty-six phonetic symbols, ten numerals and about eight punctuation marks." That Hurston gives her protagonist the sobriquet "alphabet" suggests the unlimited possibilities available in the newly opened twentieth century even to the granddaughter of a slave and the child of a rape victim. *Their Eyes Were Watching God* is a book about liberation and possibility and holiness. These themes are implicit in Janie's initials, in her nickname, and in the first page of the novel. As critic Andrew Delbanco writes in *Required Reading: Why Our American Classics Matter Now*,

> Hurston's real subject, and this is the reason her work will abide, was the universal disjunction between the limitless human imagination and the constrictions with which all human beings live their lives. She happened to know best how to exemplify this theme by writing about the lives of black women in the American South. . . . [But] she wished to honor her people by recording their uniquely tragic experi-

ence while at the same time refusing to cordon off that experience from the universal condition of hope and dread.[4]

But it is not until the death of her second husband, Joe Starks, that Janie begins to gain true freedom. For the first time in the novel since her grandmother hand-picked an aging, land-owning "skull head" for her first husband, Janie's future is not set in stone. That husband's surname, "Killicks," denotes a small anchor. Her second husband's last name, Starks, explicitly suggest the barrenness of that union.

Janie is only twenty-four when she realizes that her union with Joe is doomed. It takes her twenty years of marriage, until she is in her forties, to mount a full-scale rebellion. At his deathbed, she makes a statement that might characterize so many husband-wife relationships in the early twentieth century. She tells Joe, "You done lived wid me for twenty years and you don't half know me atall. And you could have but you was so busy worshippin' de works of yo' own hands."

After Joe's death, at almost the exact midpoint of *Their Eyes Were Watching God*, Janie reassesses her life. Images of freedom, many drawn from the first pages of the novel, return: she remembers her quest for the horizon, she burns the head rags Joe made her wear and lets her long thick braid of hair swing freely, and she herself goes "rollicking with the springtime across the world." She rediscovers the "jewel down inside herself." These images of a woman's freedom foreshadow the last half of the novel.

Her third husband, Tea Cake, bears the last name of "Woods," and he takes her to the fertile Everglades, where she can grow and thrive and find herself within a marriage that is both caring and careless. He and his name are a clear departure from the anchor of Logan Killicks and the barrenness of Joe Starks. As Mary Helen Washington writes, Janie is "a woman on a quest for her own identity and, unlike so many other questing figures in black literature, her journey would take her, not away from, but deeper and deeper into blackness, the descent into the Everglades with its rich black soil, wild cane, and communal life representing immersion into black traditions."[5]

Despite his grisly death, Vergible Woods is the right man to fulfill Janie's quest for the horizon. It is no perfect union: he beats her on occasion; he responds to the flirtatiousness of other women, notably Nunkie; and he steals money from Janie in order to gamble (returning it after he wins). But once he, too, is gone, Janie has no regrets about having married him. The ending of the novel picks up the imagery of the opening and the middle sections: "Ah done been tuh de horizon and back," Janie declares to her confidante, Pheoby Watson. Pheoby is moved by Janie's story enough that she decides she will go home and make her own husband, Sam, treat her more like an equal by taking her fishing. It is a small step, but it is clear that Hurston approves. The quest for female freedom is not fulfilled all at once: It demands seemingly insignificant increments of progress. "As much as it is a love story, *Their Eyes Were Watching God*—in its critique of black male-female relationships—is also protest literature," writes Hurston biographer Valerie Boyd. "Hurston . . . was sounding a wake-up call . . . for her own people. In *Their Eyes Were Watching God*, Hurston raised crucial feminist questions concerning the intimidation and oppression inherent in too many relationships—and she challenged black men . . . to listen and then to 'act and do things accordingly.'"[6]

In many ways, *Their Eyes* stands as a testament to Zora Neale Hurston's womanist qualities just as much as it does to Janie Crawford's. Though Hurston would probably have rejected the politics of feminism much as she rejected the politics of race, the novel is undoubtedly both political and feminist. As Washington writes, "What *Their Eyes* shows us is a woman writer struggling with the problem of the questing hero as woman and the difficulties in 1937 of giving a woman character such power and such daring."[7] Against all odds,

Hurston succeeded. Harold Bloom writes that Hurston now stands with American poet Walt Whitman as an "image of American literary vitality" and forms a part "of the American mythology of exodus, of the power to choose the party of Eros, of Life."[8] The essays that follow suggest why *Their Eyes Were Watching God* has achieved its great, if belated, success, and why Hurston and her book have both found a prominent place in the canon of great American literature.

Notes

1. Alice Walker, *In Search of Our Mothers' Gardens: Womanist Prose*. San Diego: Harcourt Brace Jovanovich, 1983, p. 7.
2. Zadie Smith, *Changing My Mind: Occasional Essays*. New York: Penguin, 2009, p. 8.
3. Langston Hughes, Arnold Rampersad, and David E. Roessel, *The Collected Poems of Langston Hughes*. New York: Knopf, 1994, p. 426.
4. Andrew Delbanco. *Required Reading: Why Our American Classics Matter Now*. New York: Farrar, Straus and Giroux, 1997, p. 206.
5. Mary Helen Washington, introduction to *Their Eyes Were Watching God*. New York: Perennial Library, 1990, p. ix.
6. Valerie Boyd, *Wrapped in Rainbows: The Life of Zora Neale Hurston*. New York: Scribner, 2003, p. 304.
7. Washington, introduction to *Their Eyes Were Watching God*, p. xiv.
8. Harold Bloom, introduction to *Zora Neale Hurston's "Their Eyes Were Watching God"*. New York: Bloom's Literary Criticism, 2008. p. 4.

Chronology

1891

Zora Neale Hurston is born on January 7 to Lucy Potts Hurston and John Hurston in Eatonville, Florida.

1917

Hurston enrolls in Morgan Academy in Baltimore, Maryland.

1918

Hurston completes high school and works as a manicurist.

1918–1919

Hurston attends Howard Preparatory School in Washington, D.C.

1919

Hurston enrolls in Howard University.

1921

Hurston publishes her first short story, "John Redding Goes to Sea," in the *Stylus*, Howard's literary magazine.

1924

The story "Drenched in Light" is published in *Opportunity*.

1925

The story "Spunk" is published in *Opportunity*.

1925–1927

Hurston studies anthropology with Franz Boas at Barnard College in New York City.

1926

Hurston begins field work for Boas.

1927

Hurston marries Herbert Sheen.

1928

Hurston graduates from Barnard with a Bachelor of Arts degree.

1930

Hurston works on the play *Mule Bone* with Langston Hughes.

1931

Hurston publishes "Hoodoo in America" in the *Journal of American Folklore*. She has a falling out with Hughes. She and Sheen divorce.

1933

Hurston publishes the story "The Gilded Six-Bits" in *Story* magazine.

1934

Hurston publishes her first novel, *Jonah's Gourd Vine*.

1935

Hurston publishes the book of folklore *Mules and Men*.

1936

Hurston uses a Guggenheim Fellowship to study folklore in the West Indies.

1937

Hurston writes *Their Eyes Were Watching God* in Haiti in seven weeks and publishes the novel on September 18.

1938

Hurston publishes *Tell My Horse*, a book of Caribbean folklore.

1939

Hurston marries Albert Price III. *Moses, Man of the Mountain* is published.

1940

Price and Hurston divorce.

1941

Hurston writes *Dust Tracks on a Road*, her autobiography.

1942

Dust Tracks on a Road is published.

1948

Seraph on the Suwanee, Hurston's last novel, is published. Hurston is falsely accused of molesting a young boy.

1949

The molestation case against Hurston is dismissed.

1950

Hurston moves back to Florida.

1956

Hurston works briefly as a librarian.

1957

She begins writing a column, Hoodoo and Black Magic, for the *Fort Pierce Chronicle*.

1958

Hurston works as a substitute teacher.

1959

Hurston suffers a stroke and later enters the St. Lucie County Welfare Home.

1960

Hurston dies on January 28. She is buried in an unmarked grave in the Garden of Heavenly Rest in Fort Pierce, Florida.

1973

Alice Walker discovers what she believes to be Hurston's grave and marks it.

1975

Walker's article "In Search of Zora Neale Hurston" is published in *Ms.* and commences a revival of interest in Hurston.

Background on
Zora Neale Hurston

The Life of Zora Neale Hurston

Kelly King Howes

Kelly King Howes writes reference books for young adults. Her book Harlem Renaissance *is a resource that presents the people, places, and times that defined an era and documents the launch of cultural development among African Americans in 1920s Harlem.*

Daughter of the three-term mayor of Eatonville, Florida, Zora Neale Hurston grew into an engaging, independent, headstrong woman and an important figure in twentieth-century literature. She attended Howard University and Barnard College (Columbia University) and had a knack for attracting some of the most brilliant minds of her time, including the famous anthropologist and Columbia professor Franz Boas, whose teaching and support promoted Hurston's career. Hurston went on to write short stories, anthologies of folktales, and novels, but she died penniless as her work fell out of favor. Her image and her works were resurrected in the 1970s with the help of renowned novelist Alice Walker, who admired Hurston and recognized her influence on other writers.

A major figure in twentieth-century African American literature, Zora Neale Hurston had a sharp wit and a vibrant personality that made her seem a natural part of the Harlem Renaissance. Stephen Watson, author of *The Harlem Renaissance*, describes her as "outrageous, unpredictable, and headstrong." Though probably best known as the author of *Their Eyes Were Watching God* (1937), Hurston was also a dedicated collector of African American folklore and one of the first writers to incorporate this rich resource into her own work. During the Harlem Renaissance she published several memorable short stories and honed the skills that would come to fruition in later years, when her novels and nonfiction works appeared. Her independent spirit and significant accomplishments made her both a model and a source of inspiration to later generations of black writers.

"Jump at de Sun"

Hurston was born in the all-black town of Eatonville, Florida, located about five miles from the larger city of Orlando. She was the fifth of eight children born to Lucy Ann Hurston, who had been a country schoolteacher, and John Hurston, a carpenter and Baptist preacher who served as mayor of Eatonville for three terms. Hurston noted in her autobiography, *Dust Tracks on a Road* (1942), that her mother treated her as a special child and encouraged her to "jump at de sun" and try to realize her dreams. Sometimes scolded by her father for her sassiness, Hurston was imaginative and curious and liked to spend time at the local country store, listening to the blues music and colorful stories played out and told by the townsfolk who gathered there.

But this comfortable life ended when Hurston was nine years old; her mother died and Hurston was sent off to attend school in a different town. Her father remarried, and Hurston didn't get along with his new wife. At fourteen she began a life of wandering, working first as a maid and then as a wardrobe assistant for a traveling theatrical company. She attended school only intermittently until she finally enrolled at Morgan Academy in Baltimore, from which she graduated in June 1918. That fall, Hurston entered Howard University in Washington, D.C., then the country's leading black college. Over the next six years, she took courses while supporting herself as a manicurist in a barber shop. It was during this period that she met Alain Locke (1886–1954), a professor of philosophy at

Howard and soon to be one of the most influential older leaders of the Harlem Renaissance.

A Promising Writer

Hurston also began writing short stories. One of these, "John Redding Goes to Sea," about a protagonist who longs to travel to faraway places, was published in the 1921 issue of *Stylus*, Howard's literary magazine. Thanks to Locke, the story came to the attention of sociologist Charles S. Johnson (1893–1956), the editor of the important black publication *Opportunity*. Johnson recognized Hurston's talent and encouraged her to move to New York City and join the other young black writers and artists who were gathering there. In January 1925 Hurston arrived in Harlem with, as she recalled in her autobiography, "$1.50, no job, no friends, and a lot of hope."

Soon Hurston's writing—as well as her lively personality—would make her a full-fledged and popular member of the Harlem Renaissance scene. She entered several of her works in *Opportunity*'s first literary contest and made a splashy appearance at the awards dinner in May when she accepted a second-place prize for a short story, "Spunk," (which would later appear in *Opportunity* and in Locke's *New Negro* anthology) and a play, "Color Struck," as well as honorable mentions for two other works. And it was at this dinner that Hurston met two important new friends: Fannie Hurst, a well-known white author, and Annie Nathan Meyer, one of the founders of Barnard College [in New York City]. Hurst soon offered Hurston a job as her secretary and chauffeur, and Meyer arranged for a scholarship so that Hurston could study anthropology at Barnard.

In the fall of 1925 Hurston entered Barnard College. She was the school's only black student. Among her teachers was the famous German-born American anthropologist Franz Boas (1858–1942), who was impressed by this dynamic young woman and saw her as the perfect person to collect the stillungathered folklore of African American culture. Hurston's studies, and especially her contact with Boas, led her to view her past and her heritage differently than she had before—to see it as something very special that might interest other people. In *Dust Tracks on a Road*, she wrote: "It was only when I was off in college, away from my native surroundings, that I could see myself like somebody else. . . . I had to have the spyglass of anthropology to look through."

Gaining Friends and a Patron

Meanwhile, Hurston had become a popular member of the younger crowd of Harlem Renaissance writers and artists, many of whom congregated at the boarding house that Hurston (known for her witty remarks) jokingly called "Niggerati Manor." She was particularly famous for her ability to tell vivid stories, complete with authentic dialect and accents. White patrons who were drawn to Harlem found Hurston very entertaining (especially those at the parties given by critic and Harlem Renaissance enthusiast Carl Van Vechten, which Hurston often attended). In fact, some of Hurston's friends felt she consciously aimed to please white listeners and friends. [Writer] Langston Hughes (1902–1967) remembered in his autobiography, *The Big Sea*, that she knew how to "represent the Negro Race" and be "a perfect 'darkie' . . . naive, childlike, sweet." In his novel *Infants of the Spring*, a fictional portrayal of the real lives and adventures of the younger Harlem Renaissance crowd, Wallace Thurman (1902–1934) cast Hurston as a character named Sweetie May Carr, who was known more "for her ribald wit and personal effervescence than for any actual literary work. She was a great favorite among those whites who went in for Negro prodigies."

As Hurston's studies at Barnard came to an end, Boas helped her get a fourteen-hundred-dollar scholarship from the Carter G. Woodson Foundation, which she used to fund a folklore-gathering trip into the southern United States. This trip was not too successful, though, because Hurston had not yet learned how to blend in with and talk to the people she interviewed; she spoke with an educated, East Coast accent that made southern blacks feel uncomfortable. Meanwhile, Hurston married Herbert Sheen in May 1927, but the marriage did not last long due to Hurston's devotion to her career above all else.

In September 1927 Hurston met Charlotte Mason (1854–1946), the wealthy white woman with a deep interest in African American culture who had already become a patron of several Harlem Renaissance writers and artists (including poet Langston Hughes and artists Miguel Covarubbias [1904–1957] and Richmond Barthé [1901–1989]). Impressed by Hurston, Mason offered to support her while she conducted her anthropological work, and in December the two women signed a contract. Hurston would receive two hundred dollars a month as well as a movie camera and a Ford automobile; she was to travel in the South and collect folklore, then report back to Mason with all the materials she had gathered.

Collecting Folklore

Hurston spent the next three years traveling—mostly in Alabama and Florida—and collected a huge amount of folklore, including songs, stories, and a careful record of the slang and figures of speech used by southern blacks. But these were also frustrating years, as Hurston failed to get any of the material published and began to doubt her ability as a writer. She also went through a painful breakup with her good friend Langston Hughes after the two had worked together on a play called *Mule Bone*, which was based on one of the folktales Hurston had collected. Hughes was deeply angered and upset when Hurston tried to get the play published as her own creation. The two friends parted company and spoke to each other only rarely for the rest of their lives.

Hurston's contract with Mason ended in 1931, but Mason continued to give her money for another year. In early 1932

Hurston went to work at Rollins College in Winter Park, Florida, where she was to create an African American arts program. Plagued by illness and a lack of money, she returned briefly to New York but finally went back to her hometown of Eatonville, Florida. This period of confusion and frustration came to an end in 1933 with the appearance of Hurston's short story, "The Gilded Six-Bits," in *Story* magazine, an event that gave her literary career a much-needed boost. Considered one of Hurston's finest stories, "The Gilded Six-Bits" concerns a young rural black couple whose happiness is temporarily disrupted by a slick city-dweller who appears in their small community. The story's well-developed characters and skillfully rendered dialect attracted the attention of the Lippincott publishing company, whose editors asked Hurston if she had written a novel. She had not, but she went right to work on one, and the result was *Jonah's Gourd Vine*, which was published by Lippincott in 1934.

Based on the lives of Hurston's parents, *Jonah's Gourd Vine* tells the story of Alabama-born John "Buddy" Pearson, the son of a former slave and, most probably, her white owner. Pearson ends up marrying three wives in succession but is unable to remain faithful to any of them. He experiences a number of ups and downs as he pursues careers as a carpenter and a preacher. Finally he seems to have achieved a happy marriage and successful life, but while returning from a business trip he has an affair with a young woman he meets on the train, and he dies before reaching home. Praised for its rich language and emotional power, *Jonah's Gourd Vine* sold well, though many critics and readers of the time failed to note the racial themes that were at its core.

Mules and Men and Other Works

Hurston's new reputation as an accomplished writer led to the publication of the collected folktales and other materials that she had always called her "story book." *Mules and Men* was published in 1935 and featured an introduction by Franz

Boas, who praised the book as helping readers understand "historically the character of American Negro life." Although everyone agreed that *Mules and Men* was important as a work of anthropology, some African American and other critics faulted Hurston for giving it too light and carefree a tone and avoiding the issue of racial conflict.

Hurston spent the next few years touring with several musical revues that were based on the folktales she had gathered, including *Sun to Sun* (produced in Florida), *The Great Day*, and *Singing Steel* (both of which appeared in Chicago). She was offered a fellowship to pursue a doctoral degree in anthropology at New York's Columbia University, but the work and study schedule proved too restrictive so she turned it down. In the fall of 1935 Hurston joined the Federal Writers Project of the newly created Works Progress Administration (WPA; a U.S. government agency founded in 1935, called the Works Progress Administration until 1939, designed to give out-of-work Americans a new start), and the next year she received a Guggenheim fellowship to collect folklore in the West Indies. Hurston published the results of her work in *Tell My Horse* (1938). After her return to the United States, she began writing a novel that would become her best-known and most acclaimed work, *Their Eyes Were Watching God*, which was published in 1937. [ED: per Chronology, this novel was written in Haiti.]

An African American Classic

The story of a woman who finds happiness by following her own heart rather than her society's expectations, *Their Eyes Were Watching God* has come to be seen as a masterpiece of African American literature. . . . The novel was praised for its warm and richly descriptive portrayal of southern black people and life, and particularly for the character of Janie, a strong, passionate, and independent woman. More than thirty years later, *Their Eyes Were Watching God* was championed by contemporary African American author Alice Walker [author of *The Color Purple*], who credited Hurston with inspiring her own work.

In the fall of 1939 Hurston became a drama instructor at North Carolina College for Negroes in Durham. She also married Albert Price III, a man at least fifteen years younger than she was (they would divorce four years later), and finished her next book, *Moses, Man of the Mountain* (1939). This novel is a retelling of the biblical story of Moses, who led the enslaved Hebrews out of Egypt and into the Promised Land of Canaan [ED: per biblical reference (Deuteronomy 3:27 and 34:4-5, Moses did NOT get to the promise land but only saw it from a mountaintop]. Hurston shaped her novel as an allegory (a symbolic representation) of African American oppression by whites. Though not considered as solid a literary achievement as her previous novel, *Moses* highlights Hurston's command of African American speech and folklore as well as her interest in conveying the history of African Americans in an unusual way.

"A Genius of the South"

Hurston spent a short period from late 1940 to early 1941 living in California with a wealthy friend, Katharine Mershon, and working on her autobiography, *Dust Tracks on a Road*, which was published in 1942. The book sold well and even won an award for contributing to better race relations. It provides an entertaining, flattering view of Hurston and is not considered entirely accurate in its facts.

At this point Hurston began to be courted by magazines such as the *Saturday Evening Post* and *Reader's Digest* for contributions. Some of the pieces she wrote for them proved controversial, though, because she seemed to suggest that blacks and whites could not live together harmoniously and should be segregated.

During the last two decades of her life Hurston continued to write but did not publish much, especially after the appearance of her final novel, *Seraph on the Suwanee,* in 1948. This novel centers on white characters (Hurston wanted to show that black writers could convey white life and people in their works), including Arvay Henson, a poor woman who gradually develops a sense of self-worth. Hurston continued to live mostly in Florida and especially enjoyed traveling up and down the Halifax and Indian rivers on her houseboat *Wanago.* But as time went by she found it increasingly difficult to support herself, and by 1950 she was forced to take a job as a maid. Over the next ten years she survived by borrowing money from friends and working for short periods as a librarian, a reporter, and a substitute teacher.

Hurston had experienced poor health for many years, and in October of 1958 she had a stroke and was forced to enter the Saint Lucie County Welfare Home, which provided long-term care for low-income people. She died on January 28, 1960, and was buried in an unmarked grave in an all-black cemetery called the Garden of Heavenly Rest in Fort Pierce, Florida. Some of Hurston's old friends took up a collection to pay for her funeral, at which the minister declared that Hurston had been wealthy despite her poverty: "The Miami paper said she died poor. But she died rich. She did something." Nearly twenty years earlier, Hurston had written in her autobiography that she had indeed "touched the four corners of the horizon."

Hurston's works were largely overlooked until the 1970s, when African American and other writers and readers began to rediscover them. A key figure in this rediscovery was novelist and poet Alice Walker, who admired Hurston's writing and independent spirit and who cited Hurston as an influence on her own work. In 1973 Walker made a pilgrimage to Florida to try to find Hurston's grave. After a long search she located what she believed to be the unmarked grave, and there she placed a marker engraved with Hurston's name and a line from a poem by Harlem Renaissance writer Jean Toomer: "A Genius of the South."

Hurston's Sense of Humor Worked Against Her

John Lowe

John Lowe is professor of English at Louisiana State University in Baton Rouge. He is the author of Jump at the Sun: Zora Neale Hurston's Cosmic Comedy *and has published many articles and essays on African American, southern, Native American, and ethnic literature, as well as pieces on humor and humor theory.*

Lowe writes that Hurston displayed a wonderful and original sense of humor, both in her personal life and in her writing. But her witty, often ribald humor worked against her and may have done much to injure her reputation. Many of those who knew deemed her jokes unladylike. In addition, they felt that Hurston joked inappropriately about using the white fascination with black culture and primitive southern life to make money off white patrons. Lowe writes that a northern bias against Hurston's reliance on recounting the southern lifestyle may have also played into contemporary attacks on Hurston. Nevertheless, Hurston continued to use humorous stories and folktales from the South and refined her techniques for evoking maximum comic effect in these tales.

The world has finally rediscovered Zora Neale Hurston. Her books are back in print, a new wave of black women writers have claimed her as their literary ancestor, and today's generation is eagerly exploring [Hurston's Florida hometown of] Eatonville and its citizens in the nation's classrooms. Zora must be somewhere, ridin' high and having the last laugh. Ap-

John Lowe, *Harlem Renaissance Re-Examined: A Revised and Expanded Edition*, ed. Victor A. Kramer and Robert A. Russ. Albany, NY: The Whitston Publishing Company, 1997, pp. 305–13. Copyright © 1997 Victor A. Kramer and Robert A. Russ. Reproduced by permission of the author.

propriately, when the *New York Times Book Review* [in 1985] published a front-page piece on Hurston, they included a great photo: Zora looks out at us, laughing, from the front seat of her Chevy, during one of her folklore collecting trips in the South.

Hurston's Humor

Why did readers turn away from this supremely gifted artist? Although Zora Neale Hurston suffered some outrageous slings and arrows for being born black and female, she also had to be silenced for her outrageous sense of humor. This no longer surprises us when one realizes the extensive role that humor plays in virtually all her works. We now know, too, thanks to [literary critic] Cheryl Wall, that Hurston pulled a really fantastic trick on the world by pretending to be ten years younger than she was; census records reveal that she was born in Eatonville, Florida, on January 7, 1891, rather than January 1, 1901. This means, among other things, that she was actually thirty-four when she entered Barnard College, although people around her thought she was in her early twenties.

This element of Hurston's personality and aesthetic did not cause her much real trouble until she arrived in New York in 1925, poised to plunge into the currents of the Harlem Renaissance. Significantly, Robert Hemenway begins his superb biography of Hurston at this critical juncture, picturing her arrival in the city in January with $1.50 in her purse, without a job or friends, "but filled with 'a lot of hope,'" carrying a bag of manuscripts, and with "the map of Florida on her tongue."

Although one would never know it from the various accounts we have of this age of "The New Negro," Hurston was part of the Harlem literati for only a few years; she looms larger in histories of the period because she represents many of the movement's best qualities. Moreover, her rapidly reappearing works now reveal her as one of the most productive, and surely one of the finest writers the group produced. Why, then, have so many scholarly studies, literary biographies by other Renaissance celebrities, and literary histories failed to do her justice? Again, one of the answers lies in how one reacts to her brand of ethnic humor.

Humor is a basic, continuing component in Hurston; to her, laughter was a way to show one's love for life, and a way to bridge the distance between author and reader. But more than this, she was determined to create a new art form based on the Afro-American cultural tradition, something she helped recover and define, as an anthropologist. I shall here analyze Hurston's concept of humor and its importance in her works, using an anthropological and literary perspective. It now seems clear that humor played a crucial role in her initial reception by, and later relations with, the other members of the Harlem Renaissance; in her sense of folklore and its functions; in the anthropological aspect of Hurston's humor, which grew out of her training as a professional folklorist; and in the ever changing and increasing role humor played in her fiction, including her masterworks, *Their Eyes Were Watching God* and *Moses, Man of the Mountain.*

Hurston's Stereotypes

Zora Hurston would quite probably be surprised to hear herself mentioned as one of the more important figures of the Harlem Renaissance; she devotes all of one paragraph to this seminal literary event in her autobiography, *Dust Tracks On a Road* (1942). Others, however, speaking of the period, have frequently noted Hurston's contagious sense of fun, her dramatic appearance, and her store of folktales, anecdotes, and jokes; all this made her a favorite at the fabled Harlem "rent" parties, salons, and gab-fests. Surprisingly, only a few writers in the group were actually from the South. Thus Zora brought a special resonance to the movement, for her "down home" qualities meshed rather well with the new interest in the so-called "primitive," a word that had much more of a cachet in the 1920s. Eventually, however, this at first refreshing quality became embarrassingly close to white stereotypes of blacks.

Unfortunately for Zora Neale Hurston, people have always found stereotypes lurking in folklore as well, and this eventually happened when her colleagues and critics began to scrutinize her fiction, which was so heavily influenced, first, by the Eatonville milieu of her childhood, and then by her anthropological studies and field work. Hurston's critics have failed to understand that stereotypes may also be positive, favorable, even overvalued, as well as negative.

Alain Locke, one of the elder statesmen of the Renaissance and one of Hurston's mentors, touched on these matters in a contribution to *The New Negro* of 1925:

> The elder generation of Negro writers expressed itself in . . . guarded idealization . . . "Be representative": put the better foot foremost, was the underlying mood. But writers like Rudolph Fisher, Zora Hurston . . . take their material objectively with detached artistic vision; they have no thought of their racy folk types as typical of anything but themselves or of their being taken or mistaken as racially representative.

Implicit in Locke's comments is a denial that rural blacks are representative of the race. Gradually, this stance began to affect the literati's view of Hurston herself; at first charmed by her wit and appearance, they began to have reservations about her "seriousness." [Critic] Sherley Anne Williams offers a sensible explanation of how this concept developed and proliferated in literary history:

> For a long time she was remembered more as a character of the Renaissance than as one of the most serious and gifted artists to emerge during this period. She was a notable taleteller, mimic, and wit, confident to the point of brashness (some might even say beyond), who refused to conform to conventional notions of ladylike behavior and middle-class decorum. To one of her contemporaries, she was the first black nationalist; to another, a handkerchief-head Uncle

Tom. . . . To Alice Walker and others of our generation, Zora was a woman bent on discovering and defining herself, a woman who spoke her own mind.

Unladylike and Opportunistic

Williams suggests that Hurston's humor was enjoyed, but found suspect, partially because it was "unladylike." Women very rarely are permitted to take on such a role, in any society. The traditional effort to place normative restrictions on women has sought the model "good girl" who is [according to scholar Greer Fox] "Chaste, gentle, gracious, ingenuous, good, clean, kind, virtuous, noncontroversial, and above suspicion and reproach." Virtually all of these communal goals for women are antithetical to the qualities associated with the humorist; it therefore comes as no surprise that women around the world almost never engage in verbal dueling or ritual insult sessions, that no female trickster or clown figure exists in the group narratives of any culture, or that the many trickster figures in world folklore are overwhelmingly male. This prejudice goes so deep that in some cultures women who laugh freely in public are considered loose, even wanton. In American society, moreover, there is a widely held belief that women generally are unable to tell jokes correctly in any case. . . .

If a woman humorist, per se, is offensive, she can only become more so if she somehow used this stance to obtain money. Much of the long-term damage to Hurston along these lines ultimately came from Wallace Thurman's *roman à clef* ["novel with a key," a book about real life disguised as fiction] of the Harlem Renaissance, *Infants of the Spring* (1932). Thurman, a sharp-tongued, bitter, but brilliant man, almost certainly felt a kind of sibling rivalry towards Hurston. His caricature of her, the figure of Sweetie Mae Carr, a leading light of "Niggerati Manor," severely damaged Hurston's literary image until Hemenway's long-needed biography corrected the picture in 1978:

Zora Neale Hurston photographed in the 1950s. © Corbis.

Sweetie Mae was a short story writer, more noted for her ribald wit and personal effervescence than for any actual literary work. She was a great favorite among those whites who went in for Negro prodigies. Mainly because she lived up to their conception of what a typical Negro should be. It seldom occurred to any of her patrons that she did this with tongue in cheek. Given a paleface audience, Sweetie Mae would launch into a saga of the little all-colored Mississippi town where she claimed to have been born. Her repertoire of tales was earthy, vulgar and funny. Her darkies always smiled through their tears. . . . Sweetie Mae was a master of southern dialect, and an able raconteur, but she was too indifferent to literary creation to transfer to paper that which she told so well. The intricacies of writing bored her, and her written work was for the most part turgid and unpolished. But Sweetie Mae knew her white folks. . . . "It's like this," she had told Raymond. "I have to eat. I also wish to finish my education. Being a Negro writer these days is a racket and I'm going to make the most of it while it lasts. Sure I cut the fool. But I enjoy it, too. . . . Thank God for this Negro literary renaissance! Long may it flourish!"

Thurman's portrait had an element of truth in it; Hurston *was* interested at this point in finding patrons—but Sweetie's coldly selfish pose is strictly a fiction.

[Poet and educator] Larry Neal's assessment of Hurston's role during the Renaissance, written a few years before the corrective of Hemenway's biography, shows how lingering the effects of reports like this were. Although he begins by stating that her reputation was perhaps hurt by "the complexity of her personality and the controversy that attended her career," he carries on the tradition by repeating all the old stories, and makes the old charges. "Miss Hurston" is said to be "very bold and outspoken, an attractive woman who had learned how to survive with native wit. . . ." Moreover,

Zora could often be an inveterate romantic [a traditional male term of derogation for women writers] . . . the historical oppression that we now associate with Southern black life was not a central aspect of her experience . . . she was

no political radical. She was, instead, a belligerent individu-
alist who was decidedly unpredictable [another favorite male
charge against women] and perhaps a little inconsistent.

Neal also accuses her, as others had before, of being "opportu-
nistic," because she had been [white author] Fannie Hurst's
secretary and [critic] Carl Van Vechten's friend. He then quotes
Langston Hughes's oft-cited dig at her, which blithely fails to
mention that Hughes himself was the benefactor of the same
white patron:

> In her youth, she was always getting scholarships and things
> from wealthy white people, some of whom simply paid her
> just to sit around and represent the Negro race for them,
> she did it in such a racy fashion. She was full of side-splitting
> anecdotes, humorous tales, and tragicomic stories, remem-
> bered out of her life in the South as the daughter of a trav-
> eling minister of God. She could make you laugh one mo-
> ment and cry the next. To many of her white friends, no
> doubt, she was a perfect "darkie," in the nice meaning they
> give the term—that is a naive, childlike, sweet, humorous,
> and highly colored Negro.

Hughes's remarks are revealing; he mentions Hurston's ability
to make people laugh, her rural background, and implies a
connection between them. He also infers that someone who is
funny and from the South therefore comes off as naive, childlike, *humorous*—as if it were a package deal. Hughes, having
arrived in Harlem from Cleveland and Washington, here seems
to share his contemporaries' stereotypes of the South and
Southern Blacks.

An Anti-Southern Bias

Using Hughes and Thurman as his expert "eye-witnesses" to
the events of the Renaissance (something many commentators
on the period have done), Neal asserts that Hurston commer-
cially popularized Black culture. He is appalled to hear a story
about Zora hosting a racially mixed party wearing a red ban-

dana—and he adds, pejoratively, "Aunt Jemima style," obviously forgetting that many other people besides Aunt Jemima wore and wear kerchiefs, especially in the South. Worst of all, she served her guests "something like collard greens and pigs' feet."

Much of the above reveals a sexist, anti-Southern bias among the intelligentsia; fairness, however, demands yet another qualification. A further factor that worked against Hurston was the residual impact of Van Vechten's *Nigger Heaven* (1926). His well-meaning but mistaken emphasis on the exotic and the sensual led him, and many readers and writers, back to old stereotypes, and caused quite a few Black writers and leaders to eschew anything that smacked of the "primitive." It was difficult for many of these people, when confronted with Zora Neale Hurston's comic folk figures, not to see parallel lines of development. Even though she dealt, for the most part, with positive elements of folk culture, they saw only stereotypes; the baby had to go out with the bathwater.

We should also remember that very few Black people of this time really understood the true greatness of Black folk culture—Hurston was one of the first writers or scientists to assess its riches and map its contours.

What led Hurston into her eventual role in Harlem and her subsequent anthropological adventures? Her autobiography, which frequently obscures rather than illuminates her past, does provide clues in this area. *Dust Tracks On a Road* won a race relations award, partly because Hurston quite consciously "accentuated the positive" and avoided bitterness, a quality she scorns in humorous, incongruous terms: "To me, bitterness is the underarm odor of wishful weakness. It is the graceless acknowledgment of defeat." One delights in the absurdity of the combination but also in the unexpected similarities we find in Hurston's equation of bitterness and underarm odor.

Making It New

This brings us to a central aspect of Hurston's humor, which is virtually identical to her greatest gift as a novelist. She truly "made it new," combining the resources of Afro-American folklore with her own fictional agenda. One of the ways she did this was by using unconventional and unexpected verbal combinations. The juxtaposition of apparently dissimilar objects or concepts is a classic cause of humor.

Similarly, as Hemenway stresses, Zora Hurston was keenly aware of the coexistent cultures of America. Indeed, throughout her text, she functions as a kind of guide and translator, initiating a presumably white reader into the mysteries of Black language and folklore.

Dust Tracks never bores the reader, largely because the book, in celebrating Zora Neale Hurston, also salutes the culture that made her. The text is larded with humor, both as structure and adornment. Hurston uses comic expressions, jokes, and entire collections of humorous effects, to amplify, underline, and sharpen the points she makes. These deceptively delightful words often contain a serious meaning, just as the slave folktales did. Hurston skillfully trims and fits folk sayings into integral parts of her narrative; on the first page, for instance, she describes her home town by saying "Eatonville is what you might call hitting a straight lick with a crooked stick. The town . . . is a by-product of something else." This type of description becomes more pungent when she combines these materials with her own imaginative coinages, as in the following description of her father's family: "Regular hand-to-mouth folks. Didn't own pots to pee in, nor beds to push 'em under. . . . No more to 'em than the stuffings out of a zero." This utterance alone gives proof to Hurston's assertion that the Negro's greatest contributions to the language were (1) the use of metaphor and simile ("hand-to-mouth folks"); (2) the use of the double descriptive ("pots . . . nor beds"); and (3) the use of verbal nouns ("stuffings").

It also reveals the way such tools can be used to revitalize language by working simultaneously in the comic mode.

Additionally, this metaphoric and frequently hyperbolic language may be combined with a comically ironic presentation of the discrepancy between appearance and reality in daily bi-racial life, as in this description of what happened when white visitors came to observe at Hurston's Black elementary school:

> We were threatened with a prompt and bloody death if we cut one caper while the visitors were present. We also sang a spiritual, led by Mr. Calhoun himself. Mrs. Calhoun always stood in the back, with a palmetto switch in her hand as a squelcher. We were all little angels for the duration, because we'd better be. She would cut her eyes and give us a glare that meant trouble, then turn her face towards the visitors and beam as much as to say it was a great privilege and pleasure to teach lovely children like us.

The description amuses, partly because of the language and tropes, also partly because (along with the narrator and the black teacher) we know the truth that is hidden from the white visitors. Another aspect of this principle may be seen in comedically sugar-coated scenes that are really put-downs of insipid white culture. When wealthy whites give the young Zora an Episcopal hymnal, she reports "some of them seemed dull and without life, and I pretended they were not there. If white people like trashy singing like that, there must be something funny about them that I had not noticed before. I stuck to the pretty ones where the words marched to a throb I could feel."

Bridging the Fictional and Real Worlds

The biggest gap, however, for the young Zora to bridge is that between her fictional/imaginary world and her real one:

> My soul was with the gods and my body in the village. People just would not act like gods. Stew beef, fried fat-back

and morning grits were no ambrosia from Valhalla. Raking back yards and carrying out chamber-pots, were not the tasks of Thor.

This momentary distaste for the real world is dispelled, however, when Zora becomes initiated into Black adult coded language on the porch of Joe Clarke's store, where the males of Eatonville congregated to swap gossip and have a "lying session," i.e., straining against each other in telling folk tales. "I would hear an occasional scrap of gossip in what to me was adult double talk, but which I understood at times. There would be, for instance, sly references to the physical condition of women, irregular love affairs, brags on male potency. . . . It did not take me long to know what was meant when a girl was spoken of as 'ruint' or 'bigged'." She was also hearing the double talk of animal tales, black interpretations of the Bible, and "tall tales." It wasn't long before she was making up her own "lies" and getting roundly chastised for it by her grandmother (surely a prototype for Nanny in *Their Eyes*), who even utters a malapropism, one of Hurston's favorite devices: "I bet if I lay my hands on her she'll stop it. I vominates a lying tongue." The forced coupling of abominate and vomit creates a delightfully expressive non-word.

Further clashes with authority receive similarly comic treatment: "I just had to talk back at established authority and that established authority hated backtalk worse than barbed-wire pie." It wasn't long, however, until Zora Neale began to see a way to be *rewarded* for her saucy imagination. Leaving home quite early, she became a governess, and soon discovered she could get out of housework by entertaining children with humorous stories; as a lady's maid for a Northern Gilbert and Sullivan company, she found out that she had a gift:

I was a Southerner, and had the map of Dixie on my tongue. . . . It was not that my grammar was bad, it was the idioms. They did not know of the way an average Southern child, white or black, is raised on simile and invective. They [southerners] know how to call names. It is an everyday affair to hear somebody called a mullet-headed, mule-eared, wall-eyed, hog-nosed, 'gator-faced, shad-mouthed, screw-necked, goat-bellied, puzzle-gutted, camel-backed, butt-sprung, battle-hammed, knock-kneed, razor-legged, box-ankled, shovel-footed, unmated so-and-so! . . . They can tell you in simile exactly how you walk and smell. They can furnish a picture gallery of your ancestors, and a notion of what your children will be like. What ought to happen to you is full of images and flavor. Since that stratum of the Southern population is not given to book-reading, they take their comparisons right out of the barnyard and the woods. When they get through with you, you and your whole family look like an acre of totem-poles.

This passage provides a deeper understanding of Hurston's comic dimensions and her conception of communal humor. It shows her awareness of the comic possibilities of accent, idiom, dialect, inflection, simile, invective, the tall tale, the boast, and comic anthropomorphism; more importantly, it suggests an awareness of the toast, the dozens, signifying, and marking, all key elements in both Afro-American culture and her fiction.

Hurston's Critics Misrepresent Her Politics

David Headon

David Headon is cultural adviser to the National Capital Authority and director of the Centre for Australian Cultural Studies in Australia. He has taught at the University of New South Wales. Among his books are North of the Ten Commandments: A Collection of Northern Territory Literature *and* The Abundant Culture: Meaning and Significance in Everyday Australia.

In this viewpoint, Headon argues that Zora Neale Hurston's many critics have distorted her true views on issues such as race and gender. For years after her death, Hurston's life and work were undervalued, in part due to the perception that she was conservative, even reactionary, on race and gender issues. While it is true, Headon writes, that she wrote and spoke some ill-phrased remarks, particularly on the subject of race, her overall life and work suggests that she was much more forward thinking than she is given credit for. Hurston's work was politically savvy, Headon maintains: It is just that her brand of politics began with the self. The central message of her life and work, Headon states, is that if one liberates oneself, all the rest will follow.

When Zora Neale Hurston, all youthful confidence and swagger, addressed the issue of race in her 1928 essay "How It Feels To Be Colored Me," she placed herself in a developing tradition of African-American social commentary stretching back to the slave narratives. Perhaps the most contentious expression of this issue before that of Hurston, [writer and educator] Alain Locke, and [poet] Langston Hughes in

David Headon, *Zora in Florida*, ed. Steve Glassman and Kathryn Lee Seidel. Gainesville: University of Central Florida Press, 1991, pp. 28–36. Copyright © 1991 by the Board of Regents of the State of Florida. Reproduced with the permission of the University Press of Florida.

the 1920s had been made by [author, activist, and scholar] W.E.B. DuBois in his *Souls of Black Folk* (1903). DuBois suggested that the "Negro" was "a sort of seventh son, born with a veil, and gifted with second-sight in this American world,—a world which yields him no true self-consciousness, but only lets him see himself through the revelation of the other world. It is a peculiar sensation, this double-consciousness, this sense of always looking at one's self through the eyes of others." Hurston, a quarter of a century later, identified no such dilemma. No "double consciousness" for her, no measuring of oneself with the tape of the white world. She declared: "I am not tragically colored. There is no great sorrow dammed up in my soul, nor lurking behind my eyes. I do not mind at all. I do not belong to the sobbing school of Negrohood who hold that nature somehow has given them a lowdown dirty deal and whose feelings are all hurt about it."

Hurston and Controversy

The parameters of the debate, then, had been established. In the decades to follow, Hurston's persistent expression of personal liberation from what she considered the misconstrued issue of race—in fiction and nonfiction alike—would ensure her a controversial status among her contemporaries. She would be resented—sometimes for good reason—and misunderstood. [Novelist] Richard Wright, reviewing *Their Eyes Were Watching God* (1937) shortly after its publication, anticipated the waning critical and community interest in Hurston in the later 1940s and 1950s when he alluded to her simple minstrel characters who "swing like a pendulum eternally in that safe and narrow orbit in which America likes to see the Negro live: between laughter and tears." It was not accurate criticism, but it was damning. And prophetic. When Hurston died in 1960, she was separated by at least a generation from her halcyon days of literary status and success. Her work, it seemed, did not reflect the growing politicization of the black community.

Not unexpectedly, during the revival of critical interest in her in the last fifteen years—a rediscovery led by [novelist] Alice Walker, [biographer] Robert Hemenway, and [poet and educator] Larry Neal, among others—Hurston's personal politics have continued to present a problem, a nettle not easily grasped. The paradoxes and contradictions, the rash generalizations and occasional braggadocio, still cannot be overlooked or ignored. How to deal with a black writer whose characters steadfastly refuse to acknowledge DuBois' "veil," characters who celebrate instead of plotting revenge, characters who want to love, discover, and transcend, rather than commit murder? How to deal with a writer whose conservatism led to an almost doctrinal anti-Communist article in the repugnant McCarthy era published in, of all places, the *American Legion Magazine*? And, most difficult of all, how to deal with a vibrant, intelligent African-American woman who, in the last pages of her 1942 biography, *Dust Tracks on the Road*, could sum up the immense human tragedy of centuries of slavery, and its particular relevance to her, in these terms: "I see nothing but futility in looking back over my shoulder in rebuke at the grave of some white man who has been dead too long to talk about. That is just what I would be doing in trying to fix the blame for the dark days of slavery and the Reconstruction. From what I can learn, it was sad. Certainly. But my ancestors who lived and died in it are dead. The white men who profited by their labor and lives are dead also. I have no personal memory of those times, and no responsibility for them." The insensitivity and culpable naïveté, even callousness, of this passage are obvious. It is devoid of a sense of history and current affairs. The cockiness is at best misplaced; at worst, it is a gross misreading of the priorities and aspirations of the black community at the time.

Little wonder that the critics, rediscovering Hurston in the 1970s and 1980s, have recoiled from her politics and her apparent lack of political acumen. Alice Walker suggests that "we are better off if we think of Zora Neale Hurston as an artist, period—rather than as the artist/politician most black writers have been required to be." For Walker, Hurston is a "*cultural revolutionary*." Larry Neal, in his 1974 profile of Hurston, summarizes the consensus critical case with this simple assertion: "One thing is clear . . . unlike Richard Wright, [Hurston] was no political radical."

Reevaluating Hurston's Politics

I want to take issue with this prevailing interpretation of Zora Neale Hurston. I propose to revise the conventional wisdom regarding the broad range of her writings, both fiction and nonfiction from 1924 to about 1950, in order to demonstrate her evolving political consciousness—individual and eccentric on occasion, yes, but perceptive and lucid, ahead of its time also. I want to show that the cutting edges of Hurston's thought have more in common with the directions of radical African-American literature of this century than has previously been recognized. While Hurston was never interested in the role of public iconoclast, her writings from 1927–28 onward confirm a steadily more trenchant awareness of the ambiguities of black/white relations, especially as this applied to the concept of "civilization." In this evolution of her political consciousness, Florida and its black population played *the* seminal role. When Hurston left Barnard to collect folklore in her home state, she had, without realizing it, embarked on a personal odyssey that would eventually lead to the adoption of a stance as potentially revolutionary in its way as that of the most militant black activist.

There are four distinct chronological stages in Hurston's development. First are the years of the young writer and scholar up to 1927, which do not show us much more than a simple joy in creation and positive sense of community. Second are 1927 and 1928, the early years of Hurston's folklore gathering in Florida, when interest in literature gives way to the excitement and discovery of the cultural mother lode confronting her in the rich imaginative lives of black people in the South. Third is the period from 1931 to 1935, when Hurston could assess more maturely the worth of her source material. Delight turns to hardened resolve and bold assertion. Political awareness ripens. In the early 1930s Hurston had the very nature and operation of Western "civilization" firmly in her sights. And fourth are the years from 1945 to 1950, Hurston's last important period of creativity, when she produced a few essays that, in their clarity and skepticism, confirmed and enlarged on the most penetrating aspects of her social critique. In my discussion I will include a cross-section of the important, but lesser known, nonfiction essays.

In "Profile" Larry Neal suggests that a "truly original" black literature will require "some new categories of perception; new ways of seeing a culture." This is a helpful starting point. Hurston does create with freshness, vigor, and originality. As I work through the stages of her political and literary development, I will make passing reference to what emerge as the six most important "new categories of perception": her recognition and celebration of the quality of black communal life—what Alice Walker in *In Search of Our Mothers' Gardens* calls her "racial health"; her emphasis on the poetry and creativity of black English; the significance she attaches to notions of personal identity and self-worth; her emergent feminist aesthetic, in natural opposition to what Walker has labeled the "Great White Western Commercial of white and male supremacy"; her suspicion of Western civilization and its machinery of cultural appropriation; and her eventual realization and articulation of the inadequacies of Western anthropological methods.

In the mid-1920s, shortly after Hurston's arrival in New York, two documents were published, less than a year apart, that were destined to assume an honored place in the literary history of this country: Alain Locke's *The New Negro* (1925) and Langston Hughes's landmark essay "The Negro Artist and the Racial Mountain" (1926). Both would have their passionate admirers and adherents, Hurston no doubt among them, and both would ultimately be accorded the prestigious title "manifesto" of the Harlem Renaissance. Significantly, both men advocated the literary potency of the black folk heritage—Locke suggesting that the folk gift could be carried "to the altitudes of art" because it did not need to fight "social battles" and right "social wrongs" and Hughes pointing to the "great field of unused material," the black "heritage of rhythm and warmth."

Early Stories

Hurston's writing at this time—short stories, prose sketches, and poems—tends to reflect the aesthetic philosophy of Locke and the passion of Hughes. The stories "Drenched in Light," published in 1924, and "Spunk," her contribution to Locke's *New Negro* anthology, are cases in point. Isie Watts, the central character in "Drenched in Light," is incorrigibly joyful. Her happiness is infectious. "Spunk," on the other hand, opens with the protagonist Spunk Banks sauntering and strutting with his married companion, Lena Kanty. Together they are, in Elijah Mosley's words, as "big as life an' brassy as tacks." Joe Kanty, Lena's humiliated husband, "that rabbit-foot colored man," is killed by Spunk, but eventually returns as a big black bobcat to haunt Spunk and finally cause his death. The fickle Eatonville townspeople, devourers of the gossip of the love triangle, figure in the story's concluding paragraph, the women eating heartily of the "funeral baked meats" and the men "[whispering] coarse conjectures between guzzles of whiskey." Eatonville life is crude, slow, deliberate; it is also a little intoxicating. But, as in the series of sketches in "The Eatonville Anthology," Hurston is content nostalgically to recall her happy childhood. Not even the death of Joe and Spunk can undermine the warm glow of memory. At this stage of her literary

Novelist, anthropologist, and African American folklorist Zora Neale Hurston beats a hountar, or mama drum, in this 1937 photograph. © Everett Collection Inc/Alamy.

career, as Hurston would later state in the introduction to *Mules and Men*, her Florida background "was fitting me like a tight chemise. I couldn't see for wearing it." She was still satisfied with the surface of things, content faithfully to reproduce the flavor of black communal life and speech. She lacked artistic—and moral—direction.

Of all the material published before Hurston's first Florida folklore-gathering trip in early 1927, the only story that anticipates the political range and achievement of her later works is the sketch entitled "Sweat," published at the end of 1926. In "Sweat" Delia Jones, a washwoman, toils relentlessly to remain with her husband, Sykes, and keep them both in food. Delia, when first married fifteen years earlier, "wuz ez pritty ez a speckled pup." As we begin the story, Delia has sweated and slaved for too many years; there is now too much "debris" cluttering "the matrimonial trail." Husband Sykes has taken a lover, whom he flaunts; he beats Delia and enjoys taunting her and playing on her fear of snakes. But he does this once too often. Revenge figures in the story's conclusion, as Sykes is killed by his own rattlesnake.

Robert Hemenway, in his fine biography of Hurston, calls "Sweat" "a story remarkably complex at both narrative and symbolic levels." He enlarges on the Freudian and Christian symbolic structure, the sophistication of the "literary design." It is a convincing interpretation, providing we endorse the tools of New Criticism. Hemenway places his emphasis where Alain Locke might have located his in the 1920s. I feel the story works more meaningfully—is more political—at the narrative and folk levels.

"Sweat" seems to be, in part, Hurston's response to Langston Hughes's imprecation to black writers in his "Racial Mountain" essay to change the old whisper "'I want to be white,' hidden in the aspirations of the black middle class of the twenties, to 'Why should I want to be white? I am a Negro—and beautiful.'" Delia Jones is beautiful—and dignified and, above all, courageous. She will not, finally, be cowed by Sykes's physical and verbal coercion. He assaults her and calls her an "ole snaggle-toothed black woman." Eventually Delia's "habitual meekness" disintegrates. Her verbal tirade, a statement of liberation, is the emotional climax of the story: "'Ah hates you, Sykes,' she said calmly. 'Ah hates you tah de same degree dat Ah *useter* love yuh. Ah done took an' took till mah belly is full up tuh mah neck . . . Ah don't wantuh see yuh 'roun' me atall. Lay 'roun' wid dat 'oman all yuh wants tuh, but gwan 'way fum me an' mah house. Ah hates yuh lak uh suck-egg dog."

In "Sweat" Zora Neale Hurston forcefully establishes an integral part of the political agenda of black literature of this century. She places at the foreground feminist questions concerning the exploitation, intimidation, and oppression inherent in so many relationships. It is not the civil rights of DuBois and [the NAACP magazine] *Crisis*, but it is civil rights nonetheless. One of Hurston's wonderful Eatonville cameo characters in "Sweat," a man named Clarke, provides the philosophical overview: "'Taint no law on earth dat kin make a man be decent if it aint in 'im. There's plenty men dat takes a wife lak dey do a joint uh sugar-cane. It's round, juicy an' sweet when dey gits it. But dey squeeze an' grind, squeeze an' grind an' wring tell dey wring *every drop* uh pleasure dat's in 'em out. When dey's satisfied dat dey is wrung dry, dey treats 'em jes lak dey do a cane-chew. Dey throws 'em away.'"

Protest Literature

"Sweat" is, in fact, protest literature. Published just before Hurston's first Florida excursion, it foreshadows, also, the far wider range of her second stage of writings—one where moral concerns take root. In a letter written in March 1927, Hurston expresses real concern at the decline of folk life and traditions in Florida's rural black communities. "Negroness," she writes "is being rubbed off by close contact with white culture." Her revitalized interest in Florida folk life had prompted her to question the coziness and tidiness of the discourse of academic life. Assumptions were no longer clear-cut, as she had been taught; she was now in the field, on the muck in Florida experiencing some of the less visible but still pervasive by-products of Western cultural appropriation.

The essay "How It Feels To Be Colored Me," published in 1928, is interesting in this context. It is almost as controversial now as when first written. One sentence in particular continues to be offensive to Hurston's readership: namely, "Slavery is the price I paid for civilization." Even Alice Walker reacts to this statement with bitter disappointment: "We can assume this was not an uncommon sentiment during the early part of this century, among black and white; read today, however, it makes one's flesh crawl." The problem, obviously, is the word "civilization." Isolated from the larger context of the essay, "civilization" appears to represent Hurston's coveted target, the implied goal of the black community at large. Up from slavery to embrace the rewards of white society. Yet, one page later in the same essay, as Hurston sits in the New World Cabaret whooping to the tempo of the "narcotic harmonies" and dancing "wildly" inside herself, she remarks that, having experienced the ecstasy of enjoyment in the music, "I creep back slowly to the veneer we call civilization. . . ." "Civilization" is now used pejoratively, connoting boredom, conservatism, apathy, and, by implication, pitifully limited cultural range.

Getting Inside African American Art

Hurston subtly undermines rather than promotes the grand myth of Western cultures—its "civilization"—the concept used most commonly to justify the barbarous excesses of European imperialism for over five hundred years. Many years later, motivated by frustration to write "My Most Humiliating Jim Crow Experience," she would take the opportunity to add her most telling remarks on this question. A white doctor treated her in a demeaning, insulting manner, prompting Hurston to reflect, rather than angrily react: "I went away," she says, "feeling the pathos of Anglo-Saxon civilization. . . . And I still mean pathos, for I know that anything with such a *false foundation* cannot last. Whom the gods would destroy, they first made mad."

Hurston had come a long way from the hero worship she accorded to some of her university professors of the mid-1920s. It was the myth of Western civilization, of course, that had constituted the very foundation stone of [American anthropologist and professor] Papa Franz Boas's anthropology courses at Barnard [College in New York City].

Freeing herself from the conditioning of the white community, she began her lone journey of personal, moral, and political discovery. It was only fitting that the catalyst should be her own turf, Florida. Letters that she wrote during the months of March and April 1928 reflect a sensibility excited and profoundly aware of the importance of her mission. She radically altered her research technique between 1927 and 1928. In her first trip, she had, as she recalled in *Dust Tracks*, "[gone] about asking, in carefully accented Barnardese, 'Pardon me, but do you know any folk-tales or folk-songs?' The men and women who had whole treasures of material just seeping through their pores looked at me and shook their heads." Hurston, the Barnard anthropologist, was fortunate enough to have been raised in the region. She knew of the existence of the treasures and could make appropriate adjustments. [Anthropologist] Margaret Mead, in Samoa, would not have the same good fortune. Nor indeed would Western anthropologists in the deserts of Australia who, thinking they were getting the words for "tree," "star," and "rock," were in fact being tricked and supplied with words describing parts of the male and female genitalia. They simply were not aware of their vulnerability; Hurston was. So she changed and began to give more of herself, be less academic, less objective. Success almost immediately followed. On March 8, 1928, she wrote a letter describing the thrill of heightened perception: "I am getting inside of Negro art and love. I am beginning to see really. . . . This is going to be big." A month later she referred to "the greatest cultural wealth of the continent" when describing black folk life. The stage was set for the stunning achievements of her third and most significant stage of writing.

Celebrating Black Life

Hurston outlined the essence of her new perceptions and insights of these years in the seven essays she included in Nancy Cunard's *Negro: An Anthology* (1934). She recalled in *Dust Tracks* her youthful need to "stretch her limbs in some mighty struggle." In the early 1930s the struggle had at last been clearly identified. The Cunard essays, on the surface detailing the originality of black art forms, go much further. At stake, for Hurston, is the crucial issue of black identity itself: self-image. So she discusses the "drama" that permeates a black person's "entire self," along with the "will to adorn," to beautify; in addition, she specifies a range of black cultural heroes and heroines. Her last essay in the group, "Spirituals and Neo-Spirituals," opens with an assertion: "The real spirituals are not really just songs." They are in fact about a whole rich, complex way of life, ranging from "sorrow songs" to celebration. Spirituals are not about glee clubs, concerts, tuxedoes, and audience hype. As Hurston points out, "The real Negro singer cares nothing about pitch. The first notes just burst out and the rest of the church joins in—fired by the same inner urge. Every man trying to express himself through song. Every man for himself." Spirituals are not entertainment, they canvas notions of freedom, confidence and self-revelation.

One of the inevitable corollaries of Hurston's promotion of the inherent quality of black life was the need to sharpen the attack on those blacks who rejected their own cultural forms, individuals who, as she put it, "ape all the mediocrities of the white brother." In 1934 she wrote an article for the *Washington Tribune* entirely devoted to the ways of the so-called black-fur-coat peerage: "Fawn as you will. Spend an eternity awe struck. Roll your eyes in ecstasy and ape the white man's every move, but until we have placed something upon his street corner that is our own, we are right back where we were when they filed our iron collar off." Hurston had finally given her political ideas prominence. It remained only for her to place something of lasting quality on art's street corner. Between 1934 and 1937 she did exactly that, in the form of one memorable short story, one extensive work of nonfiction, and one great novel. Together they comprise her most extensive political, moral, and artistic statement. The works in question are "The Gilded Six-Bits," *Mules and Men*, and *Their Eyes Were Watching God*. All three works reflect her Florida roots.

The Politics of Self

Missie May and Joe in "Six-Bits," Janie and Tea Cake in *Their Eyes Were Watching God*, the riches of folklore and hoodoo in *Mules and Men*, along with the tour-de-force description of Polk County—all exemplify Hurston's claim in *Mules and Men* concerning the "wealth and beauty of her material." She had discovered ways to combine her literary aspirations and highly individual sense of social commitment. If her popularity declined for a couple of decades, Alice Walker pinpoints why: "It seems to me that black writing has suffered, because even black critics have assumed that a book that deals with the relationships between members of a black family—or between a man and a woman—is less important than one that has white people as a primary antagonist."

Zora Hurston confronted, ultimately, the complex politics of self. In her 1945 article "Crazy for This Democracy" she attacked the hidden aspects of the Jim Crow laws: psychological manipulation (that is, whites being conditioned into believing their right to be "first by birth") and the fact that "darker people" are taught to suffer their "daily humiliations." The carefully crafted ending of "Six-Bits" exposes the complete absurdity of stereotyping; Janie's quest for self-fulfillment in *Their Eyes Were Watching God* does the same.

This is the revolutionary message of Hurston's writing: Liberate the self, and all else follows. Never succumb. In 1943 and 1950 Hurston wrote two more essays on this subject—"The 'Pet Negro' System" and "What White Publishers Won't Print"—so dominant had it become in her thinking. Her mother exhorted her when she was young to "jump at de sun." Hurston, at the peak of her artistic powers in the 1930s (and with her fertile Florida of the imagination to call on), encouraged all blacks to do the same.

Hurston Fell on Hard Times Late in Her Life

Cheryl A. Wall

Cheryl A. Wall has taught at Rutgers University. Among her books are Worrying the Line: Black Women Writers, Lineage and Literary Tradition *and* Zora Neale Hurston's "Their Eyes Were Watching God": A Casebook.

Wall investigates the late years of Hurston, taking particular note of the paradoxes in her life. For all of her fame as a writer, Hurston had to rely on working as a maid during her last decade of life. When approached by a writer, Hurston talked up her literary career and her future plans, but the reality was that she had fallen out of favor with the writing establishment as well as the reading public and was living out her life as a largely ignored has-been. In this neglected state, Hurston serves as a metaphor for all of the women writers of the Harlem Renaissance. With their works largely out of print by the 1960s, it was up to a new generation of writers, led by novelist Alice Walker, to rediscover their "mother's gardens."

On 27 March 1950, the *Miami Herald* carried a feature headlined "Famous Negro Author Working as a Maid Here Just 'to Live a Little.'" The headline introduced a series of paradoxes: the fact that a famous author was working as a maid, that domestic work represented a way to "live a little," that such an entity as a famous Negro author existed in Florida in 1950, and that fame—racially circumscribed though it was—could make so little difference in a black woman's life. The article recounted how an employer had been surprised to come across her "girl's" byline in a national magazine. "Con-

Cheryl A. Wall, *Women of the Harlem Renaissance*. Bloomington: Indiana University Press, 1995, pp. 200–04. © 1995 by Cheryl A. Wall. Reproduced by permission.

science of the Court," a short story by Zora Neale Hurston, appeared in the *Saturday Evening Post* in March 1950. Its author, who had first done domestic work as a teenager, had traveled a long way to end up where she started.

Inventing Her Life

"You can only use your mind for so long. Then you have to use your hands," a clearly abashed Hurston had explained to the journalist when he arrived to interview her. She was temporarily "written out." Although he had apparently never heard of Zora Neale Hurston, the reporter was convinced of her standing as a writer: she had published in the *Saturday Evening Post*. Charmed by her "infectious good spirits" and disarmed by her modesty, he was deaf to the contradictions in her story. She was written out, but she had recently sent a novel and three new stories to her agent. Or, she had taken this job to research the potential of establishing a magazine by and for domestic workers. Then, she had declined offers of financial help from her friends in the literary community, who had heard of her financial straits. Besides, she planned to sail for Honduras in the fall to explore the interior of that "forgotten paradise." To black Americans, she offered this article of faith: "if you do well today all that you are permitted to do, tomorrow you will be entrusted with something better."

Had the journalist, James Lyons, read the preface to [Hurston's] *Mules and Men*, he might have recognized this "feather-bed resistance" for what it was. He had asked his questions, "trying to know into somebody else's business," but she had "set something outside the door of my mind for him to play with and handle. He can read my writing but he sho' can't read my mind." Her "lies" masked the desperation of her situation; they did not protect her privacy. Instead, her lies proved so entertaining that the story was picked up by the national wire services.

Threads of truth were woven into the fabric of Hurston's lies. She had completed a new novel, but, like at least two earlier book manuscripts and the stories, it was not publishable. Her desire to explore the interior region of Honduras was rooted in reality. She had lived on the coast for almost a year while writing [her last novel] *Seraph on the Suwanee.* Her dream of discovering lost treasure in Central America was another matter. The commercial failure of the novel (a turgid melodrama of white Floridian life) helped keep this dream alive. By this time, Hurston had ample reason to prefer dreams to the realities of her life.

Engulfed in Scandal

The most bitter reality was the scandal that had engulfed her in 1948. In September, Hurston was falsely accused of molesting a ten-year-old boy, the son of the Harlem landlady who had rented her a room the previous winter. Hurston was arrested and indicted, solely on the word of her young accuser. By mid-October, the press, notably the *Baltimore Afro-American,* was onto the story as the result of a tip from a black court employee. Shocked and devastated by these events, Hurston denied the charges, presented her passport as evidence that she was in Honduras when the alleged crime occurred, wondered whether racism was the impulse behind the court's acceptance of the emotionally disturbed child's accusations, and vowed "to fight this horrible thing to the finish and clear my reputation." The case against her was finally dismissed in March 1949.

Under the circumstances, Hurston's "infectious good spirits" so noticeable a year later bespoke her steadfast refusal to be "tragically colored." In retrospect, they deepen the tragic dimension of her life. Hurston's powers as a writer had long been on the wane. Some of the essays and stories she published during the 1940s, notably "High John de Conquer" and "Story in Harlem Slang," captured the flair and the force of her earlier writing; a few essays like "Crazy for this Democracy" wrapped sophisticated political critique in the glove of folk humor, but many pieces were little more than hack work. Age, ill health, and a spiritual crisis that she experienced, perhaps while doing fieldwork in Haiti, deepened her preoccupation with spiritual matters until they became an obsession. Her iconoclastic views on race matters calcified. The pithy adages that had adorned her fiction turned into platitudes like those she offered as her credo to the *Miami Herald* reporter. While Hurston's nostrums on self-help reflected a world view as illusionary as the quest for lost treasure, their circulation in the media made their effect pernicious. Hurston spent the last ten years of her life writing a biography of [ancient Judean king] Herod the Great, which no one would read.

Hurston's Peers

To some of Hurston's critics, her life seems a metaphor for the black woman writer. The idea resonates when one considers the situation of her peers. Their work had similarly faded from view. Indeed, most of the other women writers of the Harlem Renaissance had given up their literary careers by 1950. Many had gone on to lead impressively productive lives. [Poet and fiction writer] Gwendolyn Bennett became an art teacher, director of an art center in Harlem, and, in retirement, an antiques dealer in rural Pennsylvania. After publishing a cluster of stories about a racially mixed, working-class Chicago neighborhood marked by economic conflict and cultural exchange, [writer, essayist, and playwright] Marita Bonner stopped writing in 1941; subsequently, she raised three children and taught school. After retiring as a school librarian in 1945, [poet] Anne Spencer lived, wrote, cultivated her garden, and fought for civil rights in Lynchburg [Virginia]. Like Hurston, [poet] Georgia Douglas Johnson, who worked at a series of civil service jobs following her widowhood in 1925, continued to write; her final, self-published volume of poems, *Share My World*, appeared in 1962. The ever elusive [poet]

Helene Johnson married, gave birth to a daughter, and withdrew from public life. [Poet and novelist] Jessie Fauset moved with her husband to Montclair, New Jersey, in 1939; thereafter, apart from teaching, including a semester at Hampton Institute in 1949, she limited her activity to local cultural affairs. And, for almost two decades, [novelist] Nella Larsen was employed as a nurse working the night shift at a Manhattan hospital.

But more than the inattention paid to their writing, more even than the notable productivity of their lives links Hurston to her peers. What makes Hurston's life emblematic is the capacity for self-invention that allowed her to become an artist in the first place. That capacity is depicted in the fictional representations of Joanna Marshall [a character in Fauset's *There Is Confusion*] and Clare Kendry [a character in Nella Larsen's *Passing*] and in lyric portraits such as Anne Spencer's [poem] "Lady, Lady." Their authors had also to invent themselves at a time when the terms "black," "woman," and "artist" were never complementary.

As her changes of name and identity demonstrate, Nella Larsen was continually reinventing herself. In her novels, she staged performances of identity for her protagonists, which reveal her awareness of the risks of asserting a self at odds with societal expectations, even as they expose her complicity with myths of race and gender. As she traveled from the parsonage in Philadelphia to the Pan-African conference in Paris and to Algiers, Jessie Fauset tried on the new ways of thinking that enabled her to become a writer. If, in her fiction, the values of her past prevail over these new ideas, the example she set by leaving and by writing is key. For a time, even that example appeared to be lost.

Death and Rediscovery

In the early 1960s, Hurston, Fauset, and Larsen died within four years of each other. Following a stroke, Hurston died of hypertensive heart disease on 28 January 1960 in the Saint Lucie County, Florida, welfare home. Fauset died of the same ailment in Philadelphia on 30 April 1961. A relative had taken her in after [her husband] Herbert Harris's death two years earlier, when suffering from physical infirmities and senility, Fauset was no longer able to care for herself. Nella Larsen had been dead for several days when her body was found on 30 March 1964. Her coworkers had grown concerned when she failed to report for her shift. All three women died from illnesses associated with old age. For those few people who recalled their literary careers, their writing belonged to a bygone era. None of their books was in print. If their life journeys had ended, their writing—and that of their peers—had also been consigned to the past.

Then a new generation of black women writers came of age and went, in [novelist] Alice Walker's evocative phrase, "in search of our mothers' gardens." They went in search, that is, of artistic models and a literary legacy. Individually and collectively, the biographies of the women of the Harlem Renaissance offer both models and cautionary tales. But if these literary foremothers were sometimes unable to *live* their dreams and convictions, they left a legacy in their art. Their literary legatees critique, revise, and extend the themes, forms, and metaphors that they employed in their poetry and fiction. Perhaps the most telling act of recuperation and revision is the determination of this new generation to bring to the surface those themes and plots that their precursors masked. The subtext has become the text. The lives and work of the women of the Harlem Renaissance constitute a chapter in a literary history that is in the process of being written and made.

Social Issues
in Literature

CHAPTER 2

Women's Issues in *Their Eyes Were Watching God*

Hurston's Work Can Be an Example for All Women

Ellen Cantarow

Ellen Cantarow has taught at several colleges, including the State University of New York at Old Westbury. She is the coauthor of Moving the Mountain: Women Working for Social Change *and has published articles in the* Village Voice, Grand Street, *and* Mother Jones.

In the following selection taken from a speech, Cantarow observes that Janie Crawford's bold attempt to find a life outside of traditional women's roles in society holds lessons for women of all races. Cantarow compares Janie with the female hero of Kate Chopin's The Awakening, *Edna Pontellier, a wealthy white woman in the early twentieth century who rebels from her role as wife and mother. In this comparison, Cantarow believes, Janie comes out as the stronger woman, one who forges an equal partnership with her third husband, Tea Cake. It is the type of marriage that Edna can never have and that so many women long for.*

I'd like to begin with a memory that came to my mind as I was re-reading the two books we're to discuss this morning [Kate Chopin's *The Awakening* and Zora Hurston's *Their Eyes Were Watching God*]. Two years ago, when I was teaching at SUNY [State University of New York]/Old Westbury [on Long Island], my car broke down on my way to class. I found myself in one of those high-class, desolate neighborhoods. You know. Plush desolation. No stores. Beautifully manicured streets but not a soul in sight. Hundred thousand dollar houses surrounded by fences and exquisitely tended shrubbery. A

Ellen Cantarow, "Sex, Race, and Criticism: Thoughts of a White Feminist on Kate Chopin and Zora Neale Hurston," *Radical Teacher*, September 1978, pp. 30–33. Reproduced by permission.

woman let me in at one of these houses. She looked to be in her late fifties. It was noon, but she was still dressed in a robe. She let me use her phone. And then she begged me to have coffee with her. She told me her father had just died and that she was in mourning. She told me about her husband, a corporation lawyer who was away most of the time. And she told me about her children. "I've lived for them," she said.

Intertwined Lives

The room we were sitting in was elegant. "The softest rugs and carpets covered the floors. Rich and tasteful draperies hung at doors and windows. There were paintings selected with judgment and discrimination, upon the walls." That description is lifted from *The Awakening*. It occurs when [the protagonist] Edna and [her husband] Leonce Pontellier have returned to their house in New Orleans from the vacation on Grand Isle [in Southern Louisiana] that takes up the first half of the book. The description might just as well have been of the house in Long Island, or the houses in an upper-middle-class neighborhood I grew up in in Philadelphia. I knew women like the Long Island woman while I was growing up. One was a teacher married to a neurosurgeon. Mrs. Stevens was the aunt of a friend of mine. What always struck me as odd was that while she had her own profession she said her real life was her husband and children—much as Adele Ratignolle, Edna's friend in *The Awakening*, says her life revolves around her husband and children. In her fifties Mrs. Stevens tried to commit suicide. Later she became ill. Now, she's bedridden.

Women like Mrs. Stevens were sustained in their lives by black women's labor. Black women reared such white women's children—fed them, sang to them, nurtured them. It is a black woman—a licensed practical nurse who made it to that job from being a domestic for many years—who now nurses Mrs. Stevens. Mrs. Burden's life has been different from her employer's. While Mrs. Stevens' tragedy is rooted in the dependency on her family, and the lack of self-confidence that's bound up with such dependency, Mrs. Burden's life problems have to do with continuous toil and with two unhappy marriages to men who might have been like Janie's first two husbands in *Their Eyes Were Watching God.*

Now, the reason I began with these sketches from my own experience is to point out that history has a long reach into our present lives, and to point out that the lives of white women and black women are intimately intertwined.

White Women as Ornaments

But let me come back to that and for the moment I'll turn to *The Awakening.* The reason I flashed on that morning in Long Island was because *The Awakening,* for all that it portrays Creole society [whites of European descent born in Louisiana] and a round of group swims, parties, musicales, is a very solitary sort of book. It is about Edna's isolation, her imprisonment. She's imprisoned in her marriage. She's imprisoned in the house I described earlier. She's imprisoned as a possession, a display of her husband's wealth. But if *The Awakening* is about imprisonment, it's also about the possibilities of freedom. The foil for all the images of luxurious dalliance in the summer of Grand Isle, for all the images of household luxury, is one Chopin gives us at the beginning of the book. Edna describes a walk she took in her childhood in Kentucky through a meadow: "It seemed as big as an ocean to the very little girl walking through the grass, which was higher than her waist. . . . My sunbonnet obstructed the view. I could see only the stretch of green before me, and I felt as if I must walk on forever, without coming to the end of it." Edna can see only straight ahead, neither to right nor left. The sunbonnet obstructs breadth of vision. The stretch of green goes on forever. There are no landmarks in such undifferentiated loveliness, no certain goal. Which reminds us that clear visions of liberation even forty or fifty years after Seneca Falls [an 1848 women's rights convention that initiated the suffrage movement] were very difficult if not impossible for most white middle- and upper-class women. There were those female fetters—fetters not just of clothing but of ideology—which foreclosed a world in which men like Leonce Pontellier and Robert Lebrun [a young man with whom Edna falls in love] were free to come and go as they pleased. . . .

The lack of productive work is historically significant. By 1899, when *The Awakening* was published, remunerated labor was not readily available to white women of Edna's class. Before the Civil War, the home was still a center of production, and upper-class white women really did have a role in that productivity. But by Edna's time the factory had taken over such production. Men like Leonce Pontellier were out in the world of industrial production, and captains of it. Women like Edna were the ornaments that proved a man's success in business and the professions. It's out of such history that the white women's movement of the late sixties and early seventies put such a stress on the phrase "meaningful work."

Black Women's Roles

But let's think about that phrase. Meaningful work. For black women like Mrs. Burden, work has been meaningful historically, but the meaning is very different from what I've been talking about. While Edna was being shut up in the parlor, the great grandmother of Mrs. Burden, Mrs. Stevens' nurse, and Janie's grandmother in *Their Eyes Were Watching God*, were on the auction block. The black woman was colonized. The black woman had labor imposed on her. She was used for manual labor and house service. And there was that other kind of labor: she was a "breeder woman." And she was sexually exploited by the white men whose own wives were up there on the pedestal.

This is the background for what Janie's grandmother tells her at the beginning of the novel. She's caught Janie, in the midst of Janie's own sexual awakening, kissing Johnny Taylor over the fence. She slaps her, then she sits with Janie in her lap, and half-weeping tells Janie why she wants her to get married, in a decent marriage, quickly. "De nigger woman is de mule of de world . . . Ah was born back due in slavery so it wasn't for me to fulfill my dreams of what a woman oughta be and do . . . Ah didn't want to be used for a work-ox and a brood sow and ah didn't want mah daughter used dat way neither . . . Ah wanted to preach a great sermon about colored women sittin on high but they wasn't no pulpit for me. Ah can't die easy thinkin maybe de men folks white or black is makin a spit cup outa you."

Janie Crawford's Roles

So Janie's nanny marries her off to the elderly Logan Killicks, who disgusts Janie sexually but who has a pedestal for her to stand on. To be precise, sixty acres of land and a nice house. When Joe Starks comes along down the road one day, Janie's attracted to his exuberance, his sweet talk, and a power she sees in him. So she goes off with him and marries him and for a while she lives vicariously off that power. But Joe, like Logan before him, considers Janie a possession. Like Logan, he wants her to work for, not with him. He loves what he calls her plentiful hair, but he makes her bind it up in a headrag while she minds his store. He's your complete male supremacist. At one point Janie says to him, "You sho loves to tell me whut to do, but Ah can't tell you nothin Ah see." "Dat's cause you need tellin," says Jody, "Somebody got to think for women and chillun and chickens and cows . . . they sho don't think none theirselves."

This marriage is ready for the dust bin. Like Edna, Janie's an accessory to her husband's position and work. But there are deep differences. For one thing, Janie works in Jody's general store where she finds black folk who tell the tall tales, the "lies" Hurston loved and wrote about to reclaim the roots of a people. Janie gets sustenance from that company and that culture just as Hurston did in the Eatonville where she grew up, and in her travels collecting material for her book on black folklore, for her novels, and for her books on voodoo. It's in Jody's store, not in solitary confinement, in that society among those black folk, that Janie makes her break with Jody. Someone's said she hasn't cut a plug of tobacco right. Jody says, "I god amight! A woman stay around uh store till she get as old as Methusalem and still can't cut a little thing like a plug of tobacco! Dont stand dere rollin yo pop eyes at me wid yo rump hangin nearly to yo knees!" "Then, too," Hurston's narrator continues, "Janie took the middle of the floor . . . 'Stop mixin up mah doins wid mah looks, Jody. When you git through tellin me how tuh cut uh plug uh tobacco, then you kin tell me whether mah behind is on straight or not . . . Ah aint no young gal no mo but den Ah aint no old woman neither. Ah reckon Ah looks mah age too. But ahm a woman every inch of me and ah know it. Dats a whole lot more'n *you* kin say. You big-bellies round here and put out a lot of brag, but taint nothin to it but yo big voice. Humph! Talkin bout *me* lookin old! When you pull down you britches you look lak de change uh life.' 'Great God from Zion!' gasps a bystander, 'Y'll really playin the dozens tonight.'"

The dozens [a form of African American banter]. A verbal artillery Edna doesn't have at her disposal. And there are other resources Edna doesn't have, which I'll return to in a moment. But for the minute I'll just say that between the two awakenings we're talking about today, I prefer Janie's. It's a lot better than suicide. Janie awakens to what the meaning of a white, upper-class style of marriage is, and she rejects it. She tells her friend Pheoby, "[My grandma] was borned in slavery . . . sittin on porches lak de white madam looked lak uh mighty fine thing tuh her. Dat's whut she wanted for me . . . Git up on uh high chair and sit dere. She didn't have time to think whut tuh do after you got up on de stool uh do nothin. De object wuz tuh get dere. So ah got up on de high stool lak she told me, but Pheoby, Ah done nearly languished tuh death up dere. Ah felt like de world wuz cryin' extry and Ah aint read de common news yet."

An Equal Partnership

Janie comes down off the pedestal when she stands up to Jody. And finally she's her own woman, on her own, after he dies. She meets Tea Cake, and with him she finds both companionship and sexual fulfillment. He's a gambler, a guitar player. Whites would call him shiftless. Hurston reclaims him, turns the stereotype against its creator. He should be a revelation to white readers. And so should Tea Cake and Janie's love, as opposed to all the stereotypes of black sexuality and marriage the Daniel Patrick Moynihans [American senator and sociologist who warned of the problems with nonnuclear African American families] of this country have laid on us.

But if there's one thing that mars Janie and Tea Cake's relationship, it's Tea Cake's sometimes lingering feelings that he should be the boss. At one point he beats Janie. A friend says, "Lawd! wouldn't Ah love tuh whip uh tender woman lak Janie! Ah bet she don't even holler. She just cries, eh Tea Cake? . . . mah woman would spread her lungs all over Palm Beach County [in Florida], let alone knock out my jaw teeth . . . git her good and mad, she'll wade through solid rock up to her hip pockets."

But Janie has that sort of strength, too. She fights Jody physically when she disovers he's playing around with Nunkie. Now I think Janie's psychological and physical strength come, ironically, out of precisely the experience her nanny wants to forget. It was [African American scholar and activists] W. E. B. Du Bois who captured the contradiction of black women's forced labor when he said: "Our women in black had freedom thrust contemptuously upon them. With that freedom they are buying an untrammeled independence and dear as is the price they pay for it, it will in the end be worth every taunt and groan." At one point Hurston describes Janie and Tea Cake working side by side on the muck, picking beans: "All day long the romping and playing they carried on behind the boss's back made Janie popular right away. It got the whole field to playing off and on. Then Tea Cake would help get supper afterwards."

I don't think it's accidental that the work, the sexuality, and the housework get all mixed together by Hurston here. It's a glimpse of real equality between a man and a woman in marriage. It's the kind of marriage that's impossible for Edna. And it's a glimpse on the meshing of work and marriage so much of the contemporary white women's movement has stressed. The deep partnership so many of us yearn for. It's a good possibility *Their Eyes*, in part autobiography, was wish-fulfillment. For Hurston herself, a woman on her own at home in the world, in Eatonville, in New Orleans, in Haiti, amongst the intelligentsia of Harlem, had deep conflicts between her life and her career.

Lessons for All

There is another contradiction in what I've been saying this morning. Something else that nags at me. It's that in the comparison I've been making, Edna comes off the weaker of the two women. To contemplate Janie—her resourcefulness, her fulfillment in marriage, the power of language at her disposal—to contemplate all this, and her sexuality, is to have a vicarious experience of real strength. This poses difficulties, since finally my roots aren't in the tradition Hurston is writing out of.... For counterparts to Janie in white literature I must, then, turn perhaps not to Chopin's *The Awakening*, but to [French novelist] Colette's *The Vagabond*, or to [British novelist] Doris Lessing's *The Golden Notebook*.

73

Which is to raise a final question. What am I, a white feminist journalist and critic, doing talking about Hurston's work at all? Because she gives me not just vicarious strength, but also understanding. Never, for example, can I see women like Mrs. Stevens' nurse without thinking of women like Janie. Never can I speak with black women, working- or middle-class, without considering what I've learned of black life through writing like Hurston's.

Janie Crawford Should Have the Power to Choose Her Own Life

James Robert Saunders

James Robert Saunders is a professor of English at Purdue University in West Lafayette, Indiana. He is the author of The Wayward Preacher in the Literature of African American Women *and* Tightrope Walk: Identity, Survival and the Corporate World in African American Literature. *He teaches a variety of African American literature courses.*

In the viewpoint that follows, Saunders begins by referencing an Alice Walker poem about Janie Crawford's leaving her husbands. He takes issue with this notion, claiming that Janie did not actually leave *her second husband but rather stood up to him, thus forsaking him emotionally and psychologically, after which he soon died. Saunders suggests that Walker's concept of "womanism," which she defined as "outrageous, audacious, courageous or willful behavior" on the part of a woman, is an appropriate lens through which to view Janie's actions. Janie, like Zora herself, seeks the fulfillment of her wishes and dreams. Saunders believes that in* Their Eyes Were Watching God *Hurston is primarily concerned with how women often stay in disastrous marriages but have the right to make life choices for themselves.*

Referring to Zora Neale Hurston's *Their Eyes Were Watching God* (1937), Alice Walker asserts, "There is no book more important to me than this one." Added to that statement of memorial is a poem composed by Walker dedicated to the main protagonist of that Hurston novel, a work that has rap-

James Robert Saunders, "Womanism As the Key to Understanding Zora Neale Hurston's *Their Eyes Were Watching God* and Alice Walker's *The Color Purple*," *Hollins Critic*, October 1988. Reproduced by permission.

idly become recognized as a modern classic. Included in her collection of poems entitled *Good Night, Willie Lee, I'll See You in the Morning* (1977), Walker writes:

I love the way Janie Crawford

left her husbands

the one who wanted to change her

into a mule

and the other who tried to interest her

in being a queen.

A woman, unless she submits,

is neither a mule

nor a queen

though like a mule she may suffer

and like a queen pace the floor.

Leaving Her Husbands

Within the context of that poem, Walker has accurately interpreted much of the message in Hurston's novel. Understandably, Janie is not satisfied in her marriage to Logan Killicks, especially once she discovers that he plans to work her in the fields. Yet the more subtle psychological brutality exercised by Janie's second husband Joe is equally offensive: just after having been elected mayor of Eatonville, he can be found proclaiming, "She's uh woman and her place is in de home." Upon having just met Janie, one of his initial responses to her cascading hair and light skin had been to say that "a pretty doll-baby lak you is made to sit on de front porch and rock and fan yo'self and eat p'taters dat other folks plant just special for you." It would become Starks' intention to make a lady out of one who had in his estimation been gifted with physical beauty and, hopefully, a submissive disposition.

It is worth noting that in her poem Walker indicates Hurston's heroine "left her husbands." Yet while Janie does actually leave Killicks, she forsakes Joe Starks in a much different way. Having traveled some distance to take advantage of the newly developing all-black town, that second husband soon finds himself holding all of the town's most prominent positions, including those of storekeeper, postmaster, and mayor. However, as his responsibilities begin to mount, he finally is forced to let his wife help him operate the general store. Before long, Steve Mixon, from the Eatonville community, comes into that store to get some chewing tobacco, whereupon Janie finds herself in the position of having to cut out a plug for him. She fails to do this properly, whereupon Joe issues scathing criticism and then orders, "Don't stand dere rollin' yo' pop eyes at me wid yo' rump hangin' nearly to yo' knees!" Janie is personally humiliated, but as Hurston further writes, there was in addition "laughter at the expense of women." Men milling about the store begin desecrating womanhood in general, insinuating through their hideous laughter that no woman can do things as well as men. This marks a turning point in the novel because it is the point at which Janie decides to relinquish what had been loyalty to Joe and stand up for herself. It is as though the author herself became a character in her fiction as "Janie took to the middle of the floor to talk right into Jody's face, and that was something that hadn't been done before." Thus Janie retaliates:

> "Stop mixin' up mah doings wid mah looks, Jody. When you git through tellin' me how tuh cut uh plug uh tobacco, then you kin tell me whether mah behind is on straight or not."

> "Wha—whut's dat you say, Janie? You must be out yo' head."

> "Naw, Ah ain't outa mah head neither."

> "You must be. Talkin' any such language as dat."

"You de one started talkin' under people's clothes. Not me."

"Whut's de matter wid you, nohow? You ain't no young girl to be gettin' all insulted 'bout yo' looks. You ain't no young courtin' gal. You'se uh ole woman, nearly forty."

"Yeah, Ah'm nearly forty and you'se already fifty. How come you can't talk about dat sometimes instead of always pointin' at me?"

"Tain't no use in gettin' all mad, Janie, 'cause Ah mention you ain't no young gal no mo'. No body in heah ain't lookin' for no wife outa yuh. Old as you is."

"Naw, Ah ain't no young gal no mo' but den Ah ain't no old woman neither. Ah reckon Ah looks mah age too. But Ah'm a woman every inch of me, and Ah know it. Dat's uh whole lot more'n you kin say. You big-bellies round here and put out a lot of brag, but 'tain't nothin' to it but yo' big voice. Humph! Talkin' 'bout me lookin' old! When you pull down yo' britches, you look lak de change uh life."

In this verbal exchange much of our attention is drawn to the unorthodox spellings, double negatives, and folk expressions making up black dialect. But the most important point Hurston wishes to make has to do with the manner in which Janie has responded to Joe's efforts to confine her to "her place." After twenty years of his mental abuse, she finally rejects the premise upon which he had conceived their marriage. Only in this sense has Janie actually left him, and unable ever to recover from the shock of her assertiveness, he dies from what the author tells us is some kind of kidney trouble. . . .

Womanism in the Novel

At the beginning of her collection of essays entitled *In Search of Our Mothers' Gardens,* Walker astutely offers her own list of alternative definitions for the term "womanist." The most essential explanation is that the word refers to "outrageous, audacious, courageous or willful behavior." The emphasis is on "willful" because for so long, so many black women have not been considered to be in possession of their own free wills, and no small part of the problem has resided in the psyche of black men. While many of her attitudes about the role of women in society are indeed outdated, Janie's grandmother, in *Their Eyes Were Watching God*, is not wholly out of date when she tells her ward:

> Honey, de white man is de ruler of everything as fur as Ah been able tuh find out. Maybe it's some place off in de ocean where de black man is in power, but we don't know nothin' but what we see. So de white man throw down de load and tell de nigger man tuh pick it up. He pick it up because he have to, but he don't tote it. He hand it to his womenfolks. De nigger woman is de mule uh de world so fur as Ah can see.

Nanny warns Janie about racism and sexism, but the grandmother is more specifically concerned about the position of black women at the bottom of the totem pole. In spite of this entreaty, though, Janie has to learn the lesson for herself, experiencing two marriages that resemble what life would be like in a prison. . . .

Seeking Fulfillment

It is rather difficult to believe that the similarities in these two authors' works are mere coincidence. Born in Eatonville, Florida, at some unidentified point near the turn of the century, Hurston describes in her autobiographical *Dust Tracks on a Road* (1942) how she "used to climb to the top of one of the huge chinaberry trees which guarded our front gate, and look out over the world." Young Zora Neale was anxious to behold all that a full life might afford the individual. Further on in that autobiography the author tells us, "It grew upon me that

A 2002 dress rehearsal at the Arena Stage in Washington, DC, of Zora Neale Hurston's play Polk County, *which she copyrighted in 1944 but never published or saw performed during her lifetime.* © AP Photo/Scott Suchman, Arena Stage.

I ought to walk out to the horizon and see what the end of the world was like." Similarly, in the very first line of her novel we are provided with the reflection that "Ships at a distance have every man's wish on board." Hurston then goes on to explain how some of those ships come in with the tide while others "sail forever on the horizon, never out of sight." Even those men who do not attain their dreams have at least at some point in their lives been able to envision themselves fulfilling their fantasies. At sixteen, that age when the search for identity is most profound, Janie slips out of her grandmother's house and imagines, "Oh to be a pear tree—any tree in bloom!" Janie envisions complete fulfillment; however, it must be noted that she identifies not with another person, but with a part of nature. As a "tree" she will be in possession of great strength, awesome beauty, and communion with the natural world. . . .

Searching for Zora

In the foreword to Robert Hemenway's *Zora Neale Hurston: A Literary Biography*, Walker writes of her efforts to locate and mark Hurston's grave. "It was, rather, a duty I accepted as naturally mine—as a black person, a woman, and a writer—because Zora was dead and I, for the time being, was alive." Walker's action in finding and marking Hurston's grave is comparable to the dead artist's own devotion to her craft in spite of many obstacles. . . .

In another era Hurston might have been a literary legend in her lifetime; instead, she died in relative obscurity at a Florida welfare home, based on what Walker has been able to ascertain, from either malnutrition or a stroke. Commenting on a rejection letter received by Hurston after she had submitted one of her later manuscripts, Hemenway laments that it "indicates the personal tragedy of Zora Neale Hurston: Barnard graduate, author of four novels, two books of folklore, one volume of autobiography, the most important collector of Afro-American folklore in America, reduced by poverty and circumstance." It is not so difficult to understand why Walker was compelled to find the whereabouts of Hurston's final resting place. . . .

Walker mentions that when looking for Hurston's grave, she searched and searched before finally reaching a point where there was "only one thing to do." In the midst of that desolate Florida setting, it occurred to Walker that having come this close she need only cry out for acknowledgement. "Zo-ra!" she screamed and suddenly her "foot sinks into a hole." Perhaps by some act of supernatural intervention, Hurston had "reached out" to join in communion with one who was of the same mind as she. This brings us to the point of once again considering the poem that Walker wrote in memory of Hurston's Janie Crawford. It has been noted that the poem's heroine left Logan Killicks, but her departure from Joe Starks was much more profound than mere physical leavetaking. However, even more peculiar is the fact that Hurston's character Tea Cake is not mentioned as the poet Walker tells how Janie "left her husbands." Nevertheless Tea Cake is the most significant male in Hurston's novel, being the type of natural man who seems to love Janie for herself. He and Janie work and play together, sharing their lives almost completely. Still, this presumably perfect man can strike his wife, and so she has to kill him in the end, although Hurston has made the development ambiguous by first having a rabid dog bite this third husband, causing him to go insane. Hurston has forced us, through Janie's act of self-defense, to take in the fact that some married women have had no recourse but to save themselves by violent reaction. . . .

A Woman's Right to Make Choices

It is the awe-inspiring *Their Eyes Were Watching God* that has sealed Hurston's place in arts and letters. The tale of Janie Crawford is one that was not fully appreciated during the 1930s when women were to a large extent still controlled by chauvinistic attitudes. Now, however, this landmark novel is accepted for what it is—a cornerstone in literary history. . . .

What Hurston had advocated in *Their Eyes Were Watching God* was the right of women to choose directions for themselves. "Perhaps the most important choice," say sociologists Joan Huber and Glenna Spitze, "is the ability to leave a man who will not do his share." Regardless of the changing times, there are many women who remain helplessly bound in unfulfilling matrimony. Financial dependence entraps some while others simply believe that any man is better than no man at all. It is this latter psychological phenomenon against which Hurston railed the most as she wrote her portrayal of Crawford's three fateful unions.

Janie Crawford Is Not a Feminist

Trudier Harris

Trudier Harris taught courses in African American literature and folklore at the University of North Carolina, Chapel Hill. Her books include From Mammies to Militants: Domestics in Black American Literature; Exorcising Blackness: Historical and Literary Lynching and Burning Rituals; The Power of the Porch: The Storyteller's Craft in Zora Neale Hurston, Gloria Naylor, and Randall Kenan; *and* Saints, Sinners, Saviors: Strong Black Women in African American Literature.

In this viewpoint Harris takes issue with the long line of critics and readers who view Janie Crawford as an iconic feminist figure. While acknowledging that Hurston's narration is sympathetic to the protagonist, Janie, Harris asks the reader to consider the novel from other points of view. She asserts that Janie is not heroic for leaving Logan Killicks, but that Logan treated her as any man might treat his wife during that era. Janie is also a passive character with her husbands, a victim of beatings who takes no firm action to rid herself of abusive behavior. Finally, Harris contends that because Hurston's other works are not feminist in nature, Their Eyes Were Watching God *would be an anomaly if taken as a feminist work.*

Feminist readings follow in the path of [Alice] Walker's observations on Janie in her poem "Saving the Life That Is Your Own":

I love the way Janie Crawford

left her husbands

Trudier Harris, *Approaches to Teaching Hurston's Their Eyes Were Watching God and Other Works*. New York, NY: Modern Language Association of America, 2009, pp. 69–75. © 2009 by The Modern Language Association of America. Reproduced by permission of the Modern Language Association of America.

the one who wanted to change her

into a mule

and the other who tried to interest her

in being a queen.

A woman, unless she submits,

is neither a mule

nor a queen

though like a mule she may suffer

and like a queen pace the floor.

The word "left" in Walker's poem contains the agency that I assert is missing from most of Janie's actions, and the multiplicity in "husbands" is also problematic, for it is only Logan Killicks that Janie leaves. In a riff on Walker's poem, Mary Helen Washington uses "I Love the Way Janie Crawford Left Her Husbands" as part of the title of an essay in which she asserts that Janie is more passive than active throughout *Their Eyes*, even down to the language she uses. Janie also "submits" more than she does anything else in the relationship with Jody, which suggests a voluntary relinquishing of agency that erases Walker's qualifying "unless." The comparison to mules again highlights the analogy that Hurston gave inadvertently to readings of African American female character. It is the assumption of implicit agency, however, that deserves further examination.

An Alternate View of Logan

Let's look more closely at some of the reasons that calling Janie a feminist is a superimposition on the part of readers that amounts to mere wish fulfillment. In the consideration of Janie as feminist, we seldom stop to ponder her relationship to Logan Killicks, her first husband. Students—especially undergraduates—and some scholars consistently either ignore Logan or feel that Janie is justified in leaving him. Ageism is the usual factor in denigrating Logan. How dare this old man, students seem to assert, think that Janie should be with him? He is not only old but also unromantic; in addition, his feet stink. When I ask students how old they think Logan is, they invariably place him in his late fifties or early sixties, implying that he should just die and be quiet. Their cultural backgrounds lead them to treat him almost as a child molester who deserves what he gets.

Few of them are willing to consider Janie *through* Logan's eyes. From that perspective, Janie is an ungrateful, immature little spoiled brat who cannot accept the consequences of her actions (while it is true that Nanny arranges the marriage, Janie nevertheless acquiesces in the decision—which ought to suggest something about the feminist quality of self-determination that readers like to apply to Janie). In the cultural context and historical moment from which Janie's character is drawn, African American women *did* work in the fields along with their husbands, fathers, and brothers; they plowed, sowed seed, and harvested. Yet we lock our sympathies consistently with Janie and simply dismiss Logan, which amounts to schizophrenia in our own readings. We want fulfillment for Janie, but we implicitly declare that it is inappropriate for Logan, that he has no desires that we should be inclined to respect.

What Janie wants in her first marriage is antithetical to feminist assertions that women should not be defined by or subordinated to men. Janie thus espouses the roles for women with which many traditional feminists would have trouble. Initially, Janie wants to be placed on a pedestal, pampered, and taken care of. In other words, she wants to continue in the same spoiled vein in which Nanny has raised her. That desire amounts to a questing after a kind of worship, which seems opposite to what feminists who espouse self-fulfillment would applaud. Inherent in Janie's complaints about Logan is the desire for romance, the tangible, superficial land of romance with which many movies end. Janie maintains that Logan "don't even never mention nothin' pretty" and that she "wants things sweet wid [her] marriage lak when you sit under a pear tree and think." Again, that glitter without substance is something of which many feminists would disapprove. While there is nothing inherently wrong with romance, it is not one of the primary features for self-determining feminism. Romance locates the site of fulfillment outside the self, which is grossly antithetical to the presumed feminist tenets of self-fulfillment and self-determination.

Still, undergraduate and graduate students generally celebrate when Janie leaves Logan. Then I ask them, What, precisely, has Logan done to deserve Janie's behavior toward him? I maintain that he has loved her, ignored her disrespectful attitude toward him (not just as a husband but as a human being), and allowed her more of a leisured existence than perhaps any other married woman in her neighborhood. But, students retort, he is going to buy a mule for her, which means he expects her to work outdoors, in the fields. So? What exempts her from field work? What—except the attitudes by which she is surrounded and that are implicit in her sympathetic narrative positioning? By insisting that Logan do the work outside the home while she does domestic chores, Janie is opting for traditional gender roles, traditional places in which men and women should appropriately remain. Is this feminist? Significantly, for all Janie's denigration of him, Logan is the only one of Janie's three husbands who does not beat her (though he threatens her on one occasion).

Not only does Janie leave Logan, but she is also emotionally unfaithful to him with Jody for several days before she actually departs, which raises an interesting question. Is infidelity a feminist ideal? After Janie gives Jody Starks that life-changing glass of "sweeten' water," she sneaks out to meet him during the "week or two" that he is resting in the area: "Every day after that they managed to meet in the scrub oaks across the road and talk about when he would be the big ruler of things with her reaping the benefits." Since Janie just wants romance, obviously Jody is defining the conversation, which means that Janie will be—and she is—subsumed into his vision. Perhaps it would have been less detrimental for her to stay with Logan and learn how to plow.

Janie as Passive Wife

The affair and departure with Jody raise another important issue in the consideration of Janie's so-called feminism. If Jody had not happened to walk down the road past her house, would she ever have changed her status? Would she simply have been content to denigrate Logan and continue to reap the benefits of those sixty acres that she claims she could toss over the fence acre by acre? The basic issue here is self-determination. How much gumption does Janie have to decide what her future will be—without the aid of her grandmother and some man? (But then, if she hadn't gone down the road, we would not have had the novel to discuss.) Although she holds back for a while in deciding to go with Jody, she nonetheless makes up her mind in that "week or two" that he is resting in the area. Thus she has to be persuaded—by a man—to change her life; in this instance (but *only* in this instance), Jody could be perceived as more feminist than Janie.

In terms of Janie leaving with Jody, another question arises. Is feminism a philosophy that espouses desertion and bigamy? Should we simply excuse Janie for trampling on Logan's heart? If she has treated him this way on her path to finding romance, then why should any of her lovers treat her any differently? Readers who celebrate Janie's leaving with Jody are comparable to those who sympathize with Goldilocks over the three bears. Janie and Goldilocks are the violators, not Logan Killicks and the bears. Janie treads on Logan's heart, and we ignore his pain. Yet we sympathize with her when her heart is torn to shreds as a result of Tea Cake's death. How do we justify the shifting morality that enables these dramatically different responses? (Of course, *whose* pain is dramatized in the text certainly guides our sympathies, but the troubling morality is nonetheless an issue.)

Janie's marriage to Jody, which has been much more written about than her relationship to Logan, is equally troubling from the perspective of applying a feminist reading to the novel. Janie stays with Jody for the better part of twenty years—until he dies—primarily because no man comes along to rescue her. It might reasonably be argued, therefore, that if Jody hadn't come along while Janie was married to Logan, she would have remained with Logan until he died. In other words, Janie lacks the ability to determine her own fate. She is primarily passive, which is also anathema to feminist philosophy. Feminism is about women finding ways to determine their own fates, to change their lives for their own spiritual, emotional, and financial well-being. While Janie maintains that Jody has problematic values and acts in problematic ways, she is nonetheless reaping the financial and social benefits of being "Mrs. Mayor." She is thus either a hypocrite or totally incapable of thinking for herself and making decisions that would change her life.

Let's also contemplate the matter of Jody's slapping Janie; after she prepares an almost inedible meal, "he slapped Janie until she had a ringing sound in her ears." What does she do? She simply takes it and remains in the same place in relation to Jody. While the spirit of the marriage may leave the bedroom and reside in the parlor, it still reflects a union; Janie is nonetheless still married to Jody. Of course, students might reasonably ask, What options were available to her? There are characters without partners in the text (remember Logan?), although it is not clear that divorce is an accepted or common practice. Nonetheless, if Hurston had allowed Janie to be truly embarked on a feminist quest, truly about the business of determining her own life, then options available to her might have been represented differently in the text. That Janie accepts Jody's emotional and physical violence for almost twenty years evokes comparison with her first marriage. Is Logan any uglier in behavior than Jody? Would Janie have ever made a change if Jody had not died? How feminist is passivity? How feminist is the fairy-tale "waiting for my hero to come" mode into which Janie seems to be locked for most of her life? Men and death rescue Janie; she does not rescue herself.

Janie's final strategy in dealing with her marriage to Jody is to "sav[e] up feelings for some man she had never seen." She is still passive and still in the mode of locating self-fulfillment in an exterior source. Jody slaps Janie at the seven-year mark in their marriage. She thus puts herself on hold for almost thirteen years, until Jody dies. Nanny did not want Janie to have mere "breath-and-britches" with Johnny Taylor; instead, she gets "breath-and-britches" with money with Jody Starks. He is neither "a higher bush" nor "a sweeter berry."

And lest we forget, consider that Jody slaps Janie a second time (that Hurston records; given Jody's increasing displeasure with Janie, there might have been additional occurrences as well). When Janie asserts that Jody looks like "de change uh life" when he pulls down his "britches," Jody is shocked beyond words. Shamed beyond reclamation before the men on the porch to whom he considers himself infinitely superior and turned into a perennial object of laughter, Jody does not envision a way ever to regain his swaggering status. Therefore, he "struck Janie with all his might and drove her from the store." Years of silence and "taking low" lead Janie to a verbal explosion that might have been prevented if she had developed the habit of voicing her criticisms of Jody on a regular basis. Certainly readers can point to Janie's trying to speak up against Jody on a couple of occasions and even "thrust[ing]" herself into a conversation once, but she is basically long-suffering until the scene in which she unmasks Jody's manhood and that much discussed deathbed scene in which she confronts and perhaps liberates herself from Jody. Well, it's about time. Still, it is harsh and perhaps, as [critic] Darwin T. Turner suggests, even cruel. Janie can only fully talk back to Jody for an extended period when she knows that he is no longer in control of her life; he has been leveled by illness and his imminent demise. Is it feminist, then, to triumph over the weak and dying, to make someone's exit into eternity as uncomforting as Janie makes Jody's? Is this a model of feminist human interaction? Again, our sympathies are so drawn toward Janie that we seldom contemplate the consequences of that authorial manipulation.

Tea Cake's Brutality

Perhaps the most ticklish part of considering Janie in a feminist mode is the beating she receives from Tea Cake and her response to it. It is described as "[n]o brutal beating at all. He just slapped her around a bit to show he was boss," and Janie responds lovingly to his "pett[ing]" and "pamper[ing]" of her in the fields the next day. A whupping is a whupping, no matter who delivers it and no matter how lovingly it is delivered or received. One of my favorite awful passages is the one in which the other men compliment Tea Cake on his beating of Janie:

> "Tea Cake, you sho is a lucky man," Sop-de-Bottom told him. "Uh person can see every place you hit her. Ah bet she never raised her hand tuh hit yuh back, neither. Take some uh dese ol' rusty black women and dey would fight yuh all night long and next day nobody couldn't tell you ever hit 'em. Dat's de reason Ah done quit beatin' mah woman. You can't make no mark on 'em at all. Lawd! wouldn't Ah love tuh whip uh tender woman lak Janie! Ah bet she don't even holler. She jus' cries, eh Tea Cake?"

> "Dat's right."

"See dat! Mah woman would spread her lungs all over Palm Beach County, let alone knock out mah jaw teeth. You don't know dat woman uh mine. She got ninety-nine rows uh jaw teeth and git her good and mad, she'll wade through solid rock up to her hip pockets."

The pride Tea Cake exhibits in response to their flattering observations is basically sick. And he is clear about why he considered the beating necessary; it revolves around his ownership or possession of Janie: "Ah didn't whup Janie 'cause *she* done nothin'. Ah beat her tuh show dem Turners who is boss." Since whipping Janie is a message that Tea Cake sends to the Turners, it makes Janie as much of a pawn in male competition as some other of Hurston's female characters. It is almost impossible, therefore, to build a feminist perspective on top of this set of circumstances—women are beaten (and accept those beatings) for the sake of male pride; passivity during the beating is considered a golden trait. If these are the tenets of romance that Janie so desperately desired from Logan, then it is an inherently flawed romanticism that informs her very being.

Smoothing Over Reality

That romanticism informs the language of the text. Language can smooth over objectionable actions from an acceptable character and linger unflatteringly on unpleasant words from an objectionable character. Consider the linguistic differences that surround Logan Killicks and Tea Cake Woods. Logan certainly says ugly things when he threatens to beat Janie, yet we are led to believe that his words are even more violent than the actual beatings that Janie receives from Jody and Tea Cake. Tea Cake does and says ugly things to Janie (he takes her money, beats her, and accuses her of infidelity when he is ill), but we are encouraged to forgive his transgressions, smooth over those things, because he is surrounded by the aura of romance that Janie has been seeking throughout the text. In Tea

Cake, during the time that he and Janie share good years, the form of language and the substance of language become one. Thus Hurston draws on our socialized visions of romantic relationships, to make Logan unacceptable and to encourage acceptance of Tea Cake no matter what he does before he is bitten by the dog. The romantic conceptualizations that we bring to the text make Logan seem violent without his actually committing violence and excuse Tea Cake even when he executes violence.

When that romanticism ends with Tea Cake's death, the readers who claim a feminist reading posit that Janie's shooting of Tea Cake is her ultimate act of self-determination; she chooses life instead of sacrificing herself for or to Tea Cake. I can see this interpretation, though it is kind of late in the novel for Janie to finally take a dramatic action. Still, at least she acts. What will happen *beyond* the ending of the novel, however, after she has freed herself, cannot be retrospectively applied to the novel that is just concluding.

It is important to focus for a moment or two on Tea Cake's death and the violence that brings it about. Again, through authorial manipulation, we are not allowed to contemplate the gaping surprise, the gush of blood overly long. Quickly, Tea Cake's death is relegated to the background as we are directed to Janie's grief and to her developing a defense for the white judge and jury. Tea Cake's loss is thus made small by comparison. That this man loses his life is less important than the grand funeral Janie gives for him. The symbolic love surrounding his funeral comes to mean more in the text than the fact that Tea Cake is no longer breathing and that it is Janie's shot that has stopped his breathing. Another question arises: If Tea Cake hadn't been bitten by the dog and killed by Janie, would Janie have ever been inclined—or forced—to locate self-fulfillment in some source other than men?

Yet, despite all these problematic areas, many readers—students and scholars—persist in their desire to make Janie a feminist. Even the way the narrative is told, they argue, illustrates Janie's self-determination. It is her story, they insist, and she shapes it as she desires. I have difficulty with that. Certainly Janie begins the narration, but Hurston takes over and never relinquishes those narrative reins to Janie (despite all those critical discussions about free indirect discourse and other creative methods for trying to put Janie in charge of something in the text).

Where the cracks in a feminist reading of the text widen into major breaks, or where there is no feminism at all, some scholars try to insert womanism, the concept articulated by Walker. [Literary critic] Carol P. Marsh-Lockett identifies Hurston as an African American writer who incorporates a womanist perspective into her works. However, Marsh-Lockett identifies a couple of features of womanism that appear to be inapplicable to Janie. Womanists, Marsh-Lockett asserts, are concerned about the greater good of the African American people. Janie seems to be locked into an individualistic focus that does not imply the "for the greater good" imperative of womanism. Womanism also seems to exempt Janie in its emphasis on sisterhood. She certainly does not develop any healthy sisterhood with Mrs. Turner (and that is to her credit), and the strong friendship she has with Pheoby seems totally apolitical. Issues of race, gender, and class that are inherent in womanism might surface briefly in the text, but overall perhaps womanism applies more to Hurston's other works than specifically to *Their Eyes Were Watching God*.

Hurston's Other Works

When all is said and done, there is no question that *Their Eyes Were Watching God* is a fascinating text, one that has engaged its readers from its date of publication—and it will undoubtedly continue to do so. Yet attempts to persist in reading it as a feminist text and Janie as a feminist heroine lift the novel out of Hurston's body of work, make it an aberration in comparison with her other texts. Why should Hurston have discovered feminism all of a sudden in *Their Eyes Were Watching God* when there is little evidence of it anywhere else? Female characters in her short stories are at the mercy of and are defined by men, and few of them have the prospect of heroes coming to rescue them. Delia in [Hurston's short story] "Sweat" literally sweats her life away. Missie May in "The Gilded-Six Bits" commits an (undramatized) infidelity that places her permanently at the mercy of her husband's will. Lena in [the story] "Spunk" is simply a prize for any man who is brave enough to claim her; she shares kinship with Daisy in [Hurston and Langston Hughes's play] *Mule Bone.*

When we boil *Mule Bone* down to its essence, Daisy is a pawn in the hands of black males. Despite her final dismissal of both her suitors, she is still, like Lena, the object of contest, not the initiator of it. Like females in African American trickster tales, Daisy is a prize in a contest and has value only as the award. Like [American novelist] Toni Morrison's Sweet in *Song of Solomon*, the woman's sexuality is not hers to dispense outside the approval or disapproval of the male community. And consider Arvay in [Hurston's later novel] *Seraph on the Suwanee.* Hurston is equally unable, with a white woman protagonist, to affect a feminist philosophy of representation. Arvay's husband, Jim, rapes Arvay on their wedding day (*before* the ceremony) just to show her whose property she is; she does not deviate substantially from that placement during the course of the text.

In the end, women are more often than not detached from their very bodies in Hurston's works. Babies arrive without sex, menses seldom occur, and there is little to distinguish femaleness from maleness except at the abstract emotional level. It is striking that children never appear in Hurston's fictional texts, though a baby is born in "The Gilded Six-Bits" (Hurston does include children playing games and telling stories in *Mules and Men,* her collection of folklore). The daughter in

Hurston's play *Color Struck* is an adult when we first see her. This absence could be an argument in favor of feminism (women without children trying to find themselves first), but the pattern reflects more Hurston's own desire to be free from maternal obligations; her characters are merely the beneficiaries of her desire. Still, the critical insistence on feminist intent in Hurston's works goes on.

Their Eyes Were Watching God Is About the Powerlessness of Women

Ann duCille

Ann duCille is chair of English Department and a professor of African American Studies at Wesleyan University. She is the author of The Cambridge Companion to Feminist Literary Theory *and* Skin Trade.

Although many have read Their Eyes Were Watching God *as the story of one woman's quest to find true love, duCille suggests that it is really the story of a typical black woman trapped in a patriarchal system where females have limited or no power. Thus women, duCille suggests, make the dream the truth and create their own subjective narrative in which they may prosper.* Their Eyes Were Watching God *critiques, challenges, and subverts traditional sex roles, but ultimately Janie does not win out over her male suppressors. She lives a life that is still defined by men, one in which the dominant patriarchal ideology wins out over female subjectivity.*

In *Their Eyes Were Watching God*, Nanny, who plays a major role in shaping the heroine's life, says to her sixteen-year-old granddaughter, Janie: "Dat's de very prong all us black women git hung on. Dis love! Dat's just what's got us uh pullin' and uh haulin' and sweatin' and doin' from can't see in de mornin' to can't see at night." According to a number of critics, including Hurston's principal biographer, Robert Hemenway, *Their Eyes Were Watching God* is the story of Janie Crawford's search for "dis love," for the kind of sexual fulfill-

Ann duCille, *The Coupling Convention: Sex, Text, and Tradition in Black Women's Fiction*. Oxford: Oxford University Press, Inc., 1993, pp. 116–23. © 1993 by Ann duCille. Reproduced by permission of Oxford University Press.

ment—the "organic union," to use Hemenway's term—she first experiences vicariously as a teenager watching a bee pollinate a pear blossom. From *Their Eyes*:

> [Janie] was stretched on her back beneath the pear tree soaking in the alto chant of the visiting bees, the gold of the sun and the panting breath of the breeze when the inaudible voice of it all came to her. She saw a dust-bearing bee sink into the sanctum of a bloom; the thousand sister-calyxes arch to meet the love embrace and the ecstatic shiver of the tree from root to tiniest branch creaming in every blossom and frothing with delight. So this was a marriage! She had been summoned to behold a revelation. Then Janie felt a pain remorseless sweet that left her limp and languid.

Overt Sexuality

"Dust-bearing bee," "sanctum of a bloom," "creaming," "frothing with delight"—this explicitly orgasmic imagery seems far removed from the innuendo and submerged sexuality of nineteenth-century novels. . . . At the same time, however, the use of such imagery links *Their Eyes* to a long-standing tradition of women's writing in which bees, birds, and blossoms are standard tropes [metaphors] used to signify both sexuality and the inherent inequality of heterosexual relations. [American women's rights advocate] Margaret Fuller wrote in her journal, for example: "Woman is the flower, man the bee. She sighs out of melodious fragrance, and invites the winged laborer. He drains her cup, and carries off the honey. She dies on the stalk; he returns to the hive, well fed, and praised as an active member of the community." According to [critic] Elaine Showalter, the images invoked by Fuller and such white women writers as Mary Wilkins Freeman "decoy women into slavery, yet even drowning, [women] cannot escape from their seductiveness, for to ignore their claim is also to cut oneself off from culture, from the 'humming' life of creation and achievement."

The visage of dust-bearing bees indeed serves as a decoy that lures Hurston's heroine into the seduction of orgasmic release and fantasies of matrimonial bliss. Few critics have failed to note that *Their Eyes Were Watching God* is in some way concerned with love and marriage, sex and sexuality (not necessarily in that order). The controversy over sex and the text has to do with the precise nature of that concern, with what it is that Hurston ultimately says about female independence, about sexuality, about the institution of marriage. [Critic] Michael Awkward, for example, argues that in observing the pollination of the pear blossom, Janie witnesses what "God originally intended marriage to be" and begins her own quest for such a perfect union. He suggests that Hurston likens Janie to Adam—"a signal creation without a mate." Blinded by the afterglow of her own orgasm, an overanxious Janie doesn't bother with God or ribs or dust; she fashions a mate of her own out of the first available male she sees: Johnny Taylor, the "shiftless" boy Nanny observes her kissing.

The Garden of Eden analogy is indeed implied by the text; however, I want to suggest a slight revision in what seems to me as it stands a rather masculinist reading of Janie as Adam. What Awkward calls Janie's "'pollinated' perception" of Johnny Taylor needs to be considered in light of Hurston's opening observation about the potentially destructive roles selective re-memory, illusion, and ideology play in the lives of women: "Now, women forget all those things they don't want to remember, and remember everything they don't want to forget. The dream is the truth. Then they act and do things accordingly." Hurston inverts and subverts the traditional androcentric creation myth as the first step in a woman-centered critique of the patriarchal character and perhaps the sexual disappointment of the marriage relation. While Awkward asserts that Janie witnesses what God intended marriage to be, I would argue that Janie merely *absorbs* the myth of what marriage is socially and ideologically constructed to be. Part of what *Their Eyes* confronts is the consequences for women of buying the myth, of seeking personal fulfillment in a primal male partner and equating sexual pleasure with marriage. Original sin in this text, after all, is not eating an apple proffered by woman but accepting a kiss proffered by man.

Made aware by that kiss of Janie's burgeoning womanhood and blooming sexuality, Nanny plots, in the fashion of Mrs. Bennet in [Jane Austen's] *Pride and Prejudice*, to marry her granddaughter off with all deliberate speed to a single black man in possession of a comparatively great fortune. Like Mrs. Bennet, Nanny equates male marriageability with means and property. The root of Nanny's motives, however, is more tragic than comic. A former slave with painful personal knowledge of the sexual vulnerability of black women in a male-dominated, white supremacist society, Nanny acts swiftly to save Janie from the evils of men by placing her under the "big protection" and material support of a husband. To recommend him, Logan Killicks, the groom Nanny selects, has sixty acres and "de onliest organ in town" in his parlor. Nanny does not understand, however, that at sixteen and in beautiful sexual bloom, her granddaughter is interested in the organ in a man's pants, not in his parlor. Janie wants things sweet with her marriage, "Lak when you sit under a pear tree and think." Her marriage to Logan Killicks does not "end the cosmic loneliness of the unmated." Nor does it "compel love like the sun the day." In other words, the facts of Janie's daily married life do not live up to her romantic fantasies or fulfill her sexual desires. Instead, marriage to Logan Killicks threatens to make her the very man-made mule of the world her grandmother wanted to protect her from becoming. This is the first of many disappointments, or as Hurston puts it: Janie learns from life with Logan Killicks that marriage does not make love. "Janie's first dream was dead, so she became a woman." And being a woman, in the context of this story, means creating a new dream.

Illustration of a female slave being dragged by a slave dealer. In Their Eyes Were Watching God, *it was Nanny's memory of being a slave at the mercy of white men that compelled her to persuade Janie to marry Logan Killicks. But, Ann duCille points out, Logan intended to make Janie the mule Nanny was trying to keep her from becoming.* © Bettmann/Corbis.

Creating Joe Starks

Out of the dust of bees, and pollen, and pear blossoms, Janie "creates" Joe Starks. She fashions him into the flesh-and-blood figure over which she drapes her private dream of pollination, even though she recognizes that he does not represent "sun-up and pollen and blooming trees." He calls her "pretty doll-baby" and promises her a share in the kingdom he plans to create and rule over. Janie is attracted not so much by the material promises Joe makes her as by his self-confidence, the respect he commands *like a white man*. "Dazzled" by his shirt with the silk sleeve holders and by his self-confident strut, Janie endows this "citified, stylish dressed" black man with a stature equal to that of the most important white man she knows, Mr. Washburn, her grandmother's longtime employer. Joe was a "seal-brown color," we are told, "but he acted like Mr. Washburn or somebody like that to Janie."

Janie is seduced by Joe Stark's glitter and spunk, by his "big-voice" and bravado, and by his willingness to work for her comfort in contrast to Killicks's plan to put her to work behind a plow. "You behind a plow," Joe exclaims at the idea of Janie's driving a mule. "You ain't got no mo' business wid uh plow than uh hog wid a holiday!" One might argue that Janie is attracted to Joe because of the same middle-class aspirations that will later become the source of her own brand of the bourgeois blues. As impressed by Joe's rhetoric as she is depressed by Logan's, Janie succumbs to Starks's verbal love-making. Without a good-bye or a divorce, she eases on down the road with Jody, who like the black folk hero for whom he is nicknamed, has no qualms about skipping town with another man's wife.

The great problem of this second marriage, however, is that Joe wants to command Janie like he does everyone else, to cow her like he cows the town. Janie soon learns that Joe's "big-voice" gains volume by silencing all other voices, including hers. As [critic] Sally Ferguson has noted, Janie ultimately learns what white women have known for some time: that "men who make women objects of their labor tend to treat them as things bought and owned." Janie becomes yet another of Joe's possessions. The "like a white man" walk and big talk that she initially admired in Joe become the "like a white man" domination with which she must contend. Ironically, she has traded labor behind the plow in one husband's fields for work behind the counter in another's store. In spite of herself and her grandmother, Janie becomes a mule—a "classed-off" mule, to be sure, but a mule just the same. Hurston reinforces this point by having Janie defend Matt Bonner's mule in a way she has ceased to defend herself: "They oughta be shamed uh theyselves!" she says in disgust. "Teasin' dat poor brute beast lak they is! Done been worked tuh death; done had his disposition ruint wid mistreatment, and now they got tuh finish devilin' 'im tuh deat.'" Joe overhears Janie's comments, and in a grand, magnanimous gesture he buys the mule and "frees" him. His gesture brings further ironic commentary from Janie, the meaning of which Joe misses:

> Jody, dat wuz uh mighty fine thing fuh you tuh do. 'Tain't everybody would have thought of it, 'cause it ain't no everyday thought. Freein' dat mule makes uh mighty big man outa you. Something like George Washington and Lincoln. Abraham Lincoln, he had de whole United States tuh rule so he freed de Negroes. You got uh town so you freed uh mule. You have tuh have power tuh free things and dat makes you lak uh king uh something.

Joe just beams at what he hears as praise, unaware of the bitter edge to Janie's comment on her own enslaved condition and on the condition of the townspeople Joe has cowed.

As Janie and Joe's marriage wears on, the verbal lovemaking that characterized their courtship becomes verbal assault. Janie learns to accept most insults in silence, knowing that Joe "wanted her submission" and would keep on fighting until he felt he had it. Hurston makes it clear, however, that Joe's domination and Janie's passive resistance have a devastating effect on their intimate marital relationship. "The spirit of the marriage left the bedroom and took to living in the parlor," we are told. The marital bed ceases to be a "daisy-field" for Janie and Joe to play in and becomes simply a place to sleep.

When Joe at one point slaps Janie, the smoldering discord erupts into physical violence. The slap intensifies her silent resentment, but it is a verbal attack on her womanhood that finally forces Janie to give breath to her own resistance. She tells her big-voiced husband that all he is a big voice. "You bigbellies around here and put out a lot of brag," she says, "but 'tain't nothin' to it but yo' big voice. . . . When you pull down yo' britches, you look lak de change uh life." So saying, Janie announces to his male subjects that their leader, the mighty Mayor Joe Starks, is sexually inadequate, that he can't get it up, that he's not enough man for "every inch" of woman she still is. It is significant, of course, that Janie reckons her sexuality by the male measurement of inches and makes it clear to all present that Joe's shriveled penis doesn't stand up. Hers is a series of well-placed punches that land below the belt, that not only rob Joe of "his illusion of irresistible maleness" but metaphorically feminize him by linking his impotence to female menopause—"de change uh life." In the wake of Janie's words, Joe's "vanity [bleeds] like a flood." It is a bloodletting that ultimately ends in the mayor's death, leaving Janie a financially well-fixed, independent, young widow. . . .

A System of Patriarchal Domination

Their Eyes Were Watching God is severely and profoundly critical not necessarily of heterosexual relationships in and of themselves but of the power imbalances—the relations of dominance and submission—such interactions inspire in a patriarchal society. As [critic] Hortense Spillers has written of this would-be love story: "[H]eterosexual love is neither inherently perverse nor necessarily dependence-engendering, except that the power equation between female and male tends to corrupt intimacies."

In her provocative discussion of literary matrilineage and the anxiety of influence, [critic] Dianne Sadoff describes Janie Crawford Killicks Starks Woods as a "dangerous woman"—a woman who abandons one husband, figuratively kills a second, and literally kills a third. By novel's end all of Janie's male oppressors have been eliminated, even—shockingly, for some readers—the beloved third husband, Tea Cake. However surprising his demise, Tea Cake's death at Janie's hand is a narrative necessity—what critic Susan Willis describes as the book's strongest statement, its most radical commentary on possible responses to male domination. It demonstrates, Willis suggests, that no matter how supportive the husband, "as long as relationships between men and women are embraced by a larger system in which men dominate women, no woman can expect to attain selfhood in marriage."

In another powerful feminist reading of *Their Eyes*, Hortense Spillers argues that the novel is "hurried, intense, and above all, haunted by an uneasy measure of control. One suspects that Hurston has not said everything she means but means everything she says"—that an "awful scream" has been held back. Yet for all the novel's forced "serenity," to use Spillers's word, rage resides in this text. As Sadoff notes, Hurston, however covertly, rages against male domination and ultimately liberates Janie from all men.

It is, however, not mere men who oppress in this novel but ideology—the ponderous presence of an overarching system of patriarchal domination. Janie's first and second husbands, Logan Killicks and Joe Starks, are surely agents of this patriarchal oppression, but so is her grandmother. It is, after all, Nanny who first turns Janie from the horizon and, hoping to protect her from the consequences of her own sexuality, in effect sells her into a sexual bondage sanctioned by marriage vows, even as Janie thirsts for that "foolishness" called love. Yet, if love (of men) is, as Nanny claims, "foolishness," "de very prong all us black women gits hung on," love of self, as Janie seems to have learned by novel's end, can be the prod that gets black women off the hook: the power that liberates them from the bonds of love. But where, precisely, does liberated leave them? Foregrounding the friendship between Janie and Pheoby, many feminist critics argue that such liberation as Janie achieves leaves women not alone without men but together with other women. Susan Willis, for example, suggests that the ultimate message of *Their Eyes* is not the impossibilities of heterosexual love but the possibilities of subversive sisterhood. Janie learns, according to Willis, that "although women must be with men and for men, they must also be with women and for women." For Willis, the book's "most radical single statement" comes not from Janie but from

Pheoby, who takes from the text of her friend's life a vision for altering her own marriage: "Lawd!" Pheoby says, "Ah done growed ten feet jus' listenin' tuh you, Janie. Ah ain't satisfied wid mahself no mo'. Ah means tuh make Sam take me fishing wid him after this."

But this utopian notion of "a new community based on sisterhood" seems to me more Willis's than Hurston's and gives both Janie and Pheoby more agency than the text ultimately allows them. Pheoby says she aims to make her husband take her fishing with him; she does not say she plans to make him bake bread, wash his own underwear, and iron his own shirts. Nor does she say, "Let's *you and me* go fishing, Janie." And while it is certainly a wiser Janie on whom the book closes, it is a Janie who is largely without community—female or male—and whose final thoughts are not of self but of Tea Cake, who remains the essential medium of meaning in her life and, perhaps, the last illusion.

The novel's strongest statement, I would argue, lies not in Pheoby's resolve to go fishing with her husband but in the narrator's opening observation about forgetting and remembering, which reverberates throughout the text with a sense of the power of illusion and ideology in women's lives. Within the context of the novel, it is at least in part this selective remembering—a propensity for manipulating reality and for conflating dream and truth—that stifles women's self-realization.

Janie's Powerlessness

Ultimately, then, like [critic] Mary Helen Washington, I cannot read *Their Eyes Were Watching God* as an "expression of female power," any more than I can read it as a celebration of heterosexual love. Indeed, *Their Eyes* critiques, challenges, and subverts male authority, ultimately eliminating the male oppressors, but female subjectivity does not win out over patriarchal ideology. I read this not as a failure in Hurston's fiction, as some critics do, but as its force. By way of explanation, let me underscore an important point [critic] Elliott Butler-Evans makes about Tea Cake as more patriarchal father than equal partner. When Joe Starks slaps Janie because his dinner isn't all he thinks it should be, the incident is presented by a disapproving narrator who takes the reader inside Janie's psyche and shares her reaction. Significantly, it is at this point that Janie realizes that her image of Joe has been a false one. It is here that she first sees that he "never was the flesh and blood figure of her dreams. Just something she had grabbed up to drape her dreams over." Later, however, when Tea Cake beats Janie, the narrative voice, as Butler-Evans notes, "trivializ[es] the incident in the text ('No brutal beating at all. He just slapped her around a bit to show he was boss.')"—intervening in a way that *protects* Tea Cake from being viewed as an unsympathetic character; and the community chorus clearly approves—even envies Janie—his actions.

Is narrative voice here parodic? Is part of the point the fact that society so endorses violence against women that even women themselves are conditioned—in some situations, anyway—to expect, accept, condone their own brutalization? Is Hurston demonstrating yet again how even independent-minded women can be captured, bound, diminished, and domesticated by patriarchal ideology and romantic mythology that suborne abuse in the name of "true love"? . . .

Their Eyes Were Watching God, then, is for me a novel as much about powerlessness as about power—about "women's exclusion from power," as Mary Helen Washington has suggested. It is a text as much about submission as about self-fulfillment, as much about silence as about voice. Part of the novel's force lies in its exploration of the implications and effects of patriarchal values and male domination on the lives of black women. In the course of that examination, ideology itself functions as an unnamed but nonetheless important character—a character who, more than any other, demands Janie's submission.

Convinced that she "done been tuh de horizon and back"—seen "de light at daybreak" through Tea Cake—Janie at story's end chooses not to resume the search for the horizon but to return to the world she lived in with Jody. Reinstalled in that world, she is satisfied to "set heah in mah house and live by comparisons" It is not clear, however, precisely what is being compared. What is remembered. What is forgotten.

Among the things forgotten, however, is the fact that with his last dying, rabid breath, a mad-dog Tea Cake bit Janie in the arm. "She was trying to hover him," the text says of Janie and Tea Cake's last moments together, "as he closed his teeth in the flesh of her forearm. . . . Janie struggled to a sitting position and pried the dead Tea Cake's teeth from her arm." And while critics have taken little note of this scene (which is reminiscent of Tea Cake's own encounter with a rabid dog), the implications for Janie are potentially lethal. The danger is reinforced by the statement of the doctor who attended the hydrophobic Tea Cake. He testifies at Janie's trial to finding her "all bit in the arm, sitting on the floor and petting Tea Cake's head."

In the concluding words of the novel, dream and truth merge for the last time in the image of Vergible (Truth) Tea Cake Woods prancing before Janie. "Of course he wasn't dead. He could never be dead," we are told, until Janie herself "had finished feeling and thinking. . . . She pulled in her horizon like a great fishnet. Pulled it from around the waist of the world and draped it over her shoulder." Remembering the bite of the rabid Tea Cake, however, we must wonder whether this fishnet is shawl or shroud.

Hurston's Novel Shows That Romantic Fantasy Cannot Last

Roger Rosenblatt

Roger Rosenblatt is a journalist, author, playwright, and teacher. He was also a columnist for Time *magazine. His many books include* Consuming Desires: Consumption, Culture, and the Pursuit of Happiness *and* Unless It Moves the Human Heart.

In the following viewpoint, Rosenblatt places Their Eyes Were Watching God *in the context of other African American novels. As opposed to most black literature, which pits a protagonist against the forces of white culture, Hurston's novel concerns more generally human, even self-imposed, forms of repression. Janie's chief conflict in the novel is between freedom and passion or restraint and reserve. But freedom carries with it the burdens that come along with being both African American and a woman. Her relationship with Tea Cake satisfies her need for freedom and for romance. But Rosenblatt suggests that Janie's romance with Tea Cake is unreal. They may escape the white world temporarily, but the outside world is waiting to destroy them. The idea that they can find permanent happiness, that the world is theirs, is an illusion.*

Breaking a cyclical pattern in Zora Neale Hurston's *Their Eyes Were Watching God* is not conceived of in reaction to external white forces, as it always is in [black novelist Richard] Wright, for example, but rather in opposition to various forms of repression which are more generally human, and sometimes self-manufactured. The love which the heroine, Janie, eventually achieves is her means of escape, both from the restrictive considerations of practicality and from the resultant

Roger Rosenblatt, *Black Fiction.* Cambridge, MA: Harvard University Press, 1974, pp. 85–90. Copyright © 1974 by the President and Fellows of Harvard College. Reproduced by permission of Harvard University Press.

deadness in herself. Her progress in the novel, which is opposite to the progress of almost every other black character in the literature, is toward personal freedom, yet unlike [novelist Claude] McKay's Jake in *Home to Harlem* or Bita in [McKay's] *Banana Bottom*, whose senses of personal freedom are inborn and ready-made, Janie earns that sense the hard way. She begins as a minor character in her own life story, and ends as a full-fledged heroine whose heroism consists largely of resilience.

The Plot

Born in western Florida, raised by her grandmother, Janie leads a thoroughly uneventful life until the age of sixteen. One afternoon, Janie's grandmother sees "shiftless" Johnny Taylor "lacerating her Janie with a kiss." Fearful that Janie would be ruined, as Janie's mother was ruined, she pushes Janie into marriage with Logan Killicks, and his sixty acres, who looks to Janie "like some ole skull-head in de grave yard," but to Nanny means security. "Tain't Logan Killicks Ah wants you to have, baby, it's protection." Being a slave had made Nanny a realist about a number of things: "Honey, de white man is de ruler of everything as fur as Ah been able tuh find out. Maybe it's some place way off in de ocean where de black man is in power, but we don't know nothin' but what we see. So de white man throw down de load and tell de nigger man tuh pick it up. He pick it up because he have to, but he don't tote it. He hand it to his womenfolks."

Janie marries Logan, and for a long time attempts to love him. When she finally concludes that "marriage did not make love," her "first dream was dead, so she became a woman." One evening down the road comes Jody Starks, a quick-thinking, fast-talking, ambitious man, headed for a newly founded all black community, where he plans to make his fortune. Jody offers Janie a new start. Janie takes it and marries him, committing bigamy, but soon finds herself no better off than before. True to his ambition, Jody becomes mayor of the town, and the most powerful man in the area, but just as Logan had done, he begins to treat Janie like property. Finally, "something fell off the shelf inside [Janie]. Then she went inside there to see what it was. It was her image of Jody tumbled down and shattered."

Their marriage disintegrates. Jody becomes ill and dies. On the morning of his death Janie studies her reflection in the mirror:

> The young girl was gone, but a handsome woman had taken her place. She tore off the kerchief from her head and let down her plentiful hair. The weight, the length, the glory was there. She took careful stock of herself, then combed her hair and tied it back up again. Then she starched and ironed her face, forming it into just what people wanted to see, and opened up the window and cried, "Come heah people! Jody is dead. Mah husband is gone from me."

From that point on she performs as the respectable town widow, until her third man, Tea Cake, comes into her life. Tea Cake is a completely free spirit; each of Janie's men has successively been freer than the one before. With Tea Cake Janie finds love for the first time. Their happiness ends only when Tea Cake contracts rabies after rescuing Janie and himself from a flood. Tea Cake is driven mad by the disease and when, in delirium, he goes after Janie with a gun, she shoots and kills him in self-defense. Acquitted at her trial, Janie returns to the town where she and Tea Cake had started out, observing finally that Tea Cake "wasn't dead. He could never be dead until she herself had finished feeling and thinking. The kiss of his memory made pictures of love and light against the wall. Here was peace. She pulled in her horizon like a great fishnet. Pulled it from around the waist of the world and draped it over her shoulder. So much of life in its meshes! She called in her soul to come and see."

The sea is a prominent motif in Their Eyes Were Watching God, *providing the symbols of ships viewed from a distance, the sea adapting itself to the shore, and the horizon that Janie seeks and finds when the sun is setting.* © Mirek Weichsel/First Light/Corbis.

Breaking Patterns

The images of the sea which express a certain serenity at the end of *Their Eyes Were Watching God* are used to express longing, specifically Janie's, in the first lines of the book: "Ships at a distance have every man's wish on board. For some they come in with the tide. For others they sail forever on the horizon, never out of sight, never landing until the Watcher turns his eyes away in resignation, his dreams mocked to death by Time." The Watcher in this instance is Janie, whose progress from states of longing to serenity in the novel seems largely accidental. Janie thinks of God as all-powerful, but disinterested, and credits the events, good and bad, of her life to an unchanging master-plan—"[God] made nature, and nature made everything else." As Tea Cake is dying, Janie ponders, "Somewhere up there beyond blue ether's bosom sat He. Was He noticing what was going on around here? He must because He knew everything. Did He *mean* to do this thing to Tea Cake and her?"

If it is impossible for Janie to deviate from her divine pattern, there are enough human patterns in the story available for breaking. The most binding is the prescription of her grandmother: to marry safely and well. Logan represents a sound marriage because he owns land and is therefore respectable. Jody initially appears to be a more romantic figure than Logan, but at heart is simply another, more eloquent, man of property. At a town ceremony where Jody presides over the setting up of a street lamp—"and when Ah touch de match tuh dat lamp-wick let de light penetrate inside of yuh"—a local woman bursts forth into a spiritual:

> We'll walk in de light, de beautiful light
>
> Come where the dew drops of mercy shine bright
>
> Shine all around us by day and by night
>
> Jesus, the light of the world.

The idea, with all of its usual ramifications, is that the dark needs the light. Jody may be the leader of an all-black community, but his vision for the town, and of himself, is white, and this is the vision which Janie must shake.

Marriage as a Lie

Neither Jody nor Logan is depicted as being evil. What they offer is a variety of death: passionless lives lacking any sense of creativity. Silas in "Long Black Song" ([in Richard Wright's] *Uncle Tom's Children*) is the same kind of man. Like Logan particularly, he has worked his whole life in order to own his own house. Wright put it that "he had worked hard and saved his money and bought a farm so he could grow his own crops like white men." But one day a white man, a college student, comes to his house when Silas is away, trying to sell his wife, Sarah, a combination clock and gramaphone. The white man seduces Sarah, and when Silas revenges himself, the house that he sought so long is burned to the ground with him inside of it.

The fact that Sarah allows herself to be seduced is not a sign of her promiscuity or boredom, but simply an effort at feeling human. When Silas discovers his wife's treachery, his outcry is self-condemning: "Fer ten years Ah slaved mah life out t git mah farm free." For ten years and probably more, that is, he had falsified his life, trying to be successful on standard (white) terms. Even at the end, resolving to murder his white pursuers, he decides, "Ahm gonna be hard like they is!" Sarah's marriage to him had been a lie, just as Janie's marriage to Logan and Jody were lies. For both women their marriages represented decisions to restrict themselves in the name of a kind of security which was white in color, and therefore unattainable.

Freedom Versus Passion

The conflict which Janie represents, between freedom or passion and restraint or reserve, has a special quality in black fiction. The characters who deal with this conflict often seem to be carrying on the fight at a number of different levels. . . .

As for Janie, the achievement of her freedom entails additional complications. Not only does Janie inherit the conception of the black in slavery, but of the woman in slavery as well. Remembering her grandmother's original admonition, she vents her exasperation upon Jody: "Sometimes God gits familiar wid us womenfolks too and talks His inside business. He told me how surprised He was 'bout y'all turning out so smart after Him makin' yuh different; and how surprised y'all is goin' tuh be if you ever find out you don't know half as much 'bout us as you think you do. It's so easy to make yo'self out God Almighty when you ain't got nothin' tuh strain against but women and chickens." Only Tea Cake understands the source of this outburst. Because he does understand it, it is through him that Janie discovers her pride.

This discovery, the discovery of Tea Cake himself, satisfies Janie's romanticism, which has been constant throughout the novel. Such satisfaction is a rarity in this literature, and Janie's ability to fall and stay in love, even if that love is cut short, is rarer than that. Ordinarily in black fiction, love turns out to be one-sided, not because the two people involved are not equally in love with each other, but because one of them is at the same time always trying to become successful in the sense of Jody's "success" or trying in some way to deal with the white world. . . .

A Fantasy of Independence

Their Eyes Were Watching God is structurally a simple story, yet nothing in Janie's accomplishment is simple or easy. Indeed, the enormous effort she must make in order to feel human only serves to demonstrate how strong the opposition to her humanity is. It is only when Janie and Tea Cake marry and avoid the white world entirely that they flourish. Yet we know that Janie's achievement with Tea Cake is an unreal achievement. The two of them may escape temporarily into a fantasy of independence, but like other lovers of folklore they are aware all along that there is a world outside waiting and able to destroy them. The tragedy, and the difference, is that they have been told that the world is theirs.

Janie Crawford's Narration Lends Authority to Her Story

Wendy J. McCredie

Wendy J. McCredie has taught Modern and Classical languages at Texas Lutheran University and serves as Associate Dean for Academic Affairs at Mount Mary College.

McCredie sees Their Eyes Were Watching God *in terms of Janie's continuing struggle to make her voice heard so that she can take control of her life, own it, and establish authority over her own story. The novel is broken into three phases, McCredie writes: before Janie's relationship with Tea Cake, during the relationship, and after Tea Cake's death. In the first phase, Nanny, Logan Killicks, and Joe Starks all attempt to exercise dominance over Janie by controlling her verbally. It is only with Tea Cake that Janie begins to take control of her life. Janie's narration of her story to her friend Pheoby, McCredie believes, allows her to finally fully control her own life, so that in this narration, she will live eternally in a self-authorizing present.*

Zora Neale Hurston's *Their Eyes Were Watching God* establishes a female voice of authority not only on the simple level of authorship, but also on the more complicated level of self-authorization. It is a many-voiced text that constantly folds in upon itself, repeating previous configurations that, as a result, are seen as occuring simultenously between the book's two covers. As Janie tells her story, she pulls her past, her horizon, and makes it part of herself. Her past becomes a part of her present, which is wherever she is in her narration. Thus, Janie's voice becomes the self-actualizing voice of authority. As she tells her past, she incorporates it into her

Wendy J. McCredie, "Authority and Authorization in *Their Eyes Were Watching God*," *Black American Literature Forum*, vol. 16, Spring 1982, pp. 25–28. Reproduced by permission.

present; for her present *is* the narration that her past constitutes. *Their Eyes Were Watching God* is the story of Janie's struggle to articulate, to appropriate her own voice and, through her voice, herself.

Three Phases of the Novel

There are three phases to *Their Eyes Were Watching God*: before Janie's relationship with Tea Cake, during it, and after his death (which phase includes the other two). At or near the end of each phase, Janie opens her mouth and speaks. The first time, she frees herself from Jody Starks, who has been her voice; the second, she protects herself from misunderstanding; and, with the third, she takes possession of first and second phases of herself.

Before Janie speaks effectively in the first phase, she responds to unwanted situations in two different ways. When Nanny wants to marry her off to Logan Killicks, she first verbally refuses to do so: "'Naw, Nanny, no ma'am! . . . He looks like some ole skullhead in de grave yard.'" However, this reaction only makes her grandmother more adamant about the necessity of Janie's marriage; so Janie again tries to refuse, this time without words: "The vision of Logan Killicks was desecrating the pear tree, but Janie didn't know how to tell Nanny that. She merely hunched over and pouted at the floor." Janie's inarticulateness provokes Nanny into slapping her—an action that immediately forces Janie back into childhood, where she was dependent upon her grandmother.

Nanny can relate to the child Janie's feelings as she could not a moment earlier, when she expected Janie to speak as a woman but could not accept what she had to say. Although Janie still refuses to speak, her childish inarticulateness no longer aggravates Nanny; instead, she responds to Janie on that same level of feeling:

> With her hand uplifted for the second blow she saw the
> huge tear that welled up from Janie's heart and stood in

each eye. She saw the terrible agony and the lips tightened down to hold back the cry and desisted. Instead she brushed back the heavy hair from Janie's face and stood there suffering and loving and weeping internally for both of them.

Nanny maintains the child-grandmother rapport by putting Janie on her knee and by speaking of herself in the third person: "'Come to yo' Grandma, honey. Set in her lap lak yo' use tuh. Yo' Nanny wouldn't harm a hair uh yo' head. She don't want nobody else to do it neither if she kin help it.'"

Now that Janie is a child, her grandmother has the power of speech, authority, over her. Recognizing this power, Janie pleads with Nanny not to make her marry, and if she has to marry to let her wait. She cannot directly refuse Nanny's authority, as she had earlier, for she has no voice of her own— she gave that up when she accepted the protection and comfort of Nanny's lap.

But Nanny insists that her protection will not suffice for Janie the woman. She cannot protect Janie from man, whose voice is even more authoritative than her own: "'Tain't Logan Killicks Ah wants you to have, baby, it's protection.'" Neither can Janie take on the responsibility for her own protection, for she is cut off from her past, her author(iz)ing:

> ". . . you ain't no everyday chile like most of 'em. You ain't got no papa, you might jus' as well say no mama, for de good she do yuh. You ain't got nobody but me. And mah head is ole and tilted towards de grave. Neither can you stand alone by yo'self."

After this speech, Janie gives in to Nanny, again inarticulately—she bursts out sobbing. Nanny quickly cements her authority by recounting her past, which also proves that, although she could protect Janie's mother when Leafy was a child, Nanny could not protect her daughter once she had become a woman. Janie will marry Logan Killicks.

Marriage to Logan Killicks

With Logan, Janie goes through a process similar to the one she went through with her grandmother. At the end, however, instead of giving in to his voice, she acts on her feelings, establishing, if not her own voice, at least her independence from the past which deprived her of authority. After they are married, Logan attempts to get Janie to work alongside him on the farm. At first, she refuses. But then she gives in as she had with Nanny, except this time she articulates her acceptance of another's authority: "'Ah'll cut de p'taters fuh yuh.'" She has established the effectiveness of her own voice. Logan, however, resents this independence on her part, and again Janie is confronted with her past which allows her no authority:

> "Youse powerful independent around here sometime considerin'." "Considerin' whut for instance?" "Considerin' youse born in a carriage 'thout no top to it, and yo' mama and you bein' born and raised in de white-folks backyard."

Nevertheless, Logan cannot destroy Janie's new articulateness.

When she talks about the possibility of leaving him, he recognizes that this is a real possibility; but he cannot admit that to her, since that would grant her a power he has just refused to recognize:

> There! Janie had put words to his held-in fears. She might run off sure enough. The thought put a terrible ache in Logan's body, but he thought it best to put on scorn. . . . "Ah'm sleepy. Ah don't aim to worry mah gut into a fiddlestring wid no s'posin'."

The next morning, Logan attempts to establish his authority by ordering Janie to help him. She refuses and Logan accuses her "of her mama, her grandmama and her feelings, and she couldn't do a thing about any of it." Instead of fighting back at him with words, Janie acts. Just feeling, she turns from the door and then carefully considers what her husband has just told her, along with the "other things she had seen and heard." Although she now has a voice, it has no recognized authority behind it. Her feelings, her inarticulateness, are what force her to act, not her voice. Realizing that she will never escape her nonauthoritative past while living with Logan, she decides to begin a new life in a new place with, perhaps, a new man: "A feeling of sudden newness and change came over her. Janie hurried out of the front gate and turned south. Even if Joe [Starks] was not there waiting for her, the change was bound to do her good." Janie cuts herself off completely from her past, hoping that doing so will facilitate the establishment of her own voice: "Her old thoughts were going to come in handy now, but new words would have to be made and said to fit them." The next line, however, indicates what the true nature of her new life will be: "'Green Cove Springs,' he told the driver. So they were married there before sundown, just like Joe had said. With new clothes of silk and wool."

Janie and Joe Starks

Janie becomes the prize possession of Mr. Joe Starks, mayor of Eatonville. In his belated welcoming speech, Tony Taylor makes her position awfully clear when he lists Janie along with Jody's store and land: "'Brother Starks, we welcomes you and all dat you have seen fit tuh bring amongst us—yo' belov-ed wife, yo' store, yo' land—.'" When the crowd demands a speech from Janie, Jody tells the townspeople that his "'wife don't know nothin' 'bout no speech-makin'. Ah never married her for nothin' lak dat. She's uh woman and her place is in de home.'" Later, he explains to Janie that "'Ah told you in de very first beginnin' dat Ah aimed tuh be uh big voice. You oughta be glad, 'cause dat makes uh big woman outa you.'" As Jody's possession, it is as unnatural for Janie to speak as it would be for his store or his land to do so. Anything she has to say must be said through her husband.

For a while, Janie remains an inarticulate possession. She desires speech, but endures speechlessness, knowing that her talking-out will simply provoke Jody: "'. . . Ah hates disagreement and confusion,'" she reasons, "'so Ah better not talk. It makes it hard tuh git along'." The first time she does speak, she thinks no one hears her. She grumbles about the men's mistreatment of Tony's rundown mule. But Jody, overhearing her, stops the men with his authoritative voice and buys the mule to protect it from further abuse. After this act, all the men congratulate Jody, who they feel has done a fine thing. Even Janie congratulates him, crediting him for her feelings. Jody, in effectively articulating Janie's words, which expressed her feelings, rises even higher in the town's esteem, while Janie continues to be enveloped by her husband's authoritarianism.

Jody's actions to save the mule are emblematic of his actions with Janie. Having taken her away from Logan to protect her from overwork, Jody treats her as a possession that, as such, contributes to the respect others pay him. And since Jody cannot afford to lose that respect, Janie must maintain herself above the others: She cannot speak to them, nor can she laugh with them. Jody calls this isolation protection. When Janie asks to go to the mule's "funeral,"

> Joe was struck speechless for a minute. "Why, Janie! You wouldn't be seen at uh draggin'-out wouldja? Wid any and everybody in uh passle pushin' and shovin' wid they no-manners selves? Naw, naw!" "You would be dere wid me, wouldn't yuh?" "Dat's right, but Ah'm uh man even if Ah is de Mayor. But de mayor's wife is somethin' different again. Anyhow they's liable tuh need me tuh say uh few words over de carcass, dis bein' uhspecial case. But you ain't goin' off in all dat mess uh commonness. Ah'm surprised at yuh fuh askin'."

Speechless Possession

Even though Janie recognizes Joe's authority over her—she asks, not demands or states—and his protection of her, she still cannot do as she pleases.

This section of Janie's story, Hurston brackets between lines of separating dots as if to emphasize it as a distinct subphase within the book's ten beginning chapters, which, taken together, constitute the first phase of the novel. Within this section, Janie accepts her position as Starks' wife, becoming a speechless, protected possession who bows down to his authority in the same way the rest of the town does. In doing so, however, she gains nothing. Until Jody's death, Janie will, with important exceptions, refrain from expressing her feelings:

> ... gradually, she pressed her teeth together and learned to hush. . . . She wasn't petal-open anymore with him. . . . She found that she had a host of thoughts she had never expressed to him, and numerous emotions she had never let Jody know about. Things packed up and put away in parts of her heart where he could never find them. She was saving up feelings for some man she had never seen. She had an inside and an outside now and suddenly she knew how not to mix them.

And when Janie does display her pent-up emotions by speaking back to Jody, he is so taken aback that he is speechless and resorts to a physical expression of feeling, rather than an articulate one of authority:

> Janie had robbed him of his illusion of irresistible maleness that all men cherish . . . . But Janie had done worse, she had cast down his empty armor before men and they had laughed, would keep on laughing. When he paraded his possessions hereafter, they would not consider the two together. They'd look with envy at the things and pity the man that owned them . . . . And the cruel deceit of Janie! Making all that show of humbleness and scorning him all the time! Laughing at him, and now putting the town up to do the same. Joe Starks didn't know the words for all this, but he knew the feeling. So he struck Janie with all his might and drove her from the store.

By speaking out, Janie robs Joe of his unquestioned authority in the town, which depended upon the identification of his possessions, of which Janie was one. Janie establishes her independence from his voice and causes the death of that voice for the rest of the town. The next time Janie speaks her feelings to Jody, he is on his death bed. He dies listening to Janie's voice.

Jody's death gives Janie her longed-for freedom from another's authority, and the one-way protection and possession that went with it. She finds, however, that she cannot enjoy her independence for long. Other men, drawn by the desire to possess her property and professing her need for protection, gather on the store porch. But, until Tea Cake, none of them talks about feelings or sharing or playing. Tea Cake, on the other hand, "wanted her to play . . . thought it natural for her to play."

Janie and Tea Cake

Chapter 10, in which Tea Cake introduces himself to Janie and establishes himself as one of her admirers though not yet as a suitor, functions as a transitional chapter between the first and second phases of *Their Eyes Were Watching God*. At the end of Chapter 11, Janie accepts Tea Cake's company in a passage which sets the tone for their future relationship:

> "Well, all right, Tea Cake, Ah wants tuh go wid you real bad, but,—oh, Tea Cake, don't make no false pretense wid me!"
> "Janie, Ah hope God may kill me, if Ah'm lyin'. Nobody else on earth kin hold uh candle tuh you, baby. You got de keys to de kingdom."

It takes both Janie and Tea Cake a while to trust each other, and themselves, enough to do without pretenses; but after Janie refuses protection from Tea Cake's friends in Jacksonville and Tea Cake refuses possession of Janie's money in Orlando, they set off for the "muck" in the Everglades. At first,

Janie stays at home, cooking and cleaning as she had with Logan and Jody; then, as she had with them also, she begins to work—but not for Tea Cake, with him; not to earn more money or to possess more, but to be with Tea Cake, to love more; not because Tea Cake demands that she do so, but because he asks her to.

The first fight Janie and Tea Cake have occurs because Janie is jealous of another woman, Nunkie, who is flirting with Tea Cake. Janie, acting on her feelings as she had with both Logan and Jody, confronts Nunkie and Tea Cake in the cane, demanding an explanation for their being there. Tea Cake explains, Nunkie runs off, and Janie goes home. She is not driven out of the fields as she had been driven out of Jody's store; she chooses to go. When Tea Cake comes home, she reacts the same way she had in the fields—she feels, she acts, and, then, she speaks:

> She walked slowly and thoughtfully to the quarters. It wasn't long before Tea Cake found her there and tried to talk. She cut him short with a blow and they fought from one room to the other, Janie trying to beat him, and Tea Cake kept holding her wrists and wherever he could to keep her from going too far. "Ah b'lieve you been messin 'round her!" she panted furiously. "No sich uh thing!" Tea Cake retorted. "Ah b'lieve yuh did." "Don't keer how big uh lie get told, somebody kin b'lieve it!" They fought on.

Unlike her previous confrontations, Janie's fight with Tea Cake ends not with an estrangement but with a renewal of their love for each other:

> The next morning Janie asked like a woman, "You still love ole Nunkie?" "Naw, never did, and you know it too. Ah didn't want her." "Yeah, you did." She didn't say this because she believed it. She wanted to hear his denial. She had to crow over the fallen Nunkie. "Whut would Ah do wid dat lil chunk of a woman wid you around? She ain't good for nothin' exceptin' tuh set up in uh corner by de kitchen stove

and break wood over her head. You'se something tuh make uh man forgit tuh git old and forgit tuh die."

The next season, however, the roles are reversed and Tea Cake beats Janie:

> Everybody talked about it next day in the fields. It aroused a sort of envy in both men and women. The way he petted and pampered her as if those two or three face slaps had nearly killed her made the women see visions and the helpless way she hung on him made men dream dreams.

The community recognizes, through its manifestation as a beating, the love that belongs to Janie and Tea Cake. And both Tea Cake and Janie gain respect, although for different reasons—Janie for being a fine submissive wife, and Tea Cake for possessing and being able to protect such a wife (Tea Cake does not beat Janie for anything she has done but to protect her from Mrs. Turner's brother). By beating her, Tea Cake establishes a claim on Janie. He warns off intruders while assuaging his own jealousy as Janie had done the season before:

> . . . he had whipped Janie. Not because her behavior justified his jealousy, but it relieved that awful fear inside him. Being able to whip her reassured him in possession. "Ah wouldn't be knockin' her around. Ah didn't wants whup her last night, but ol' Mis' Turner done sent for her brother tuh come tuh bait Janie in and take her way from me. Ah didn't whup Janie 'cause she done nothin'. Ah beat her tuh show dem Turners who is boss."

The first season, Janie establishes her right of possession over Tea Cake's love; the second season, Tea Cake establishes his right over hers. The first fight is for themselves, and the second for the outside world that only recognizes man's, Tea Cake's, authority to possess and protect woman.

"Killing" Her Husbands

The third confrontation Janie has with Tea Cake corresponds to the last one she had with Jody: She "kills" both of them, one with her words and the other with her actions, in order that she may survive, either figuratively or literally; there is no reason to hold her culpable for the death of either man. When Janie goes into the sick room to talk to Jody, she realizes he is not there; instead, it is Joe who "gave her a ferocious look. A look with all the unthinkable coldness of outer space. She must talk to a man who was ten immensities away." Likewise, the man who, driven mad by rabies, later points a pistol at her, is not really Tea Cake, for "Tea Cake was gone. Something else was looking out of his face." But underlying these instructive correspondences are equally instructive differences: Jody dies because he cannot survive recognizing, and having the town recognize, that Janie is an independent person, whereas Tea Cake dies as a result of his protecting Janie from the attack of a rabid dog. Jody dies after finding out that Janie never belonged to him, Tea Cake after refusing to surrender Janie to death. The one tries to smother Janie's voice, the other to save it.

As in her first fight with Tea Cake, her shooting him is motivated by a selfish feeling—in this case, fear for her life: She "saw the ferocious look in his eyes and went mad with fear . . . . She threw up the barrel of the rifle in frenzied hope and fear. Hope that he'd see it and run, desperate fear for her life." She acts on her feelings as a human being, not on her feelings regarding Tea Cake, whom she still loves but who no longer exists in the crazed body that threatens her life. After she has shot him, though, she expresses her love wordlessly:

> Janie held his head tightly to her breast and wept and thanked him wordlessly for giving her the chance for loving service. She had to hug him tight for soon he would be gone, and she had to tell him for the last time. Then the grief of outer darkness descended.

It is only at her trial that Janie articulates her love for Tea Cake—in order to protect herself from misunderstanding: "It was not death she feared. It was misunderstanding. If they made a verdict that she didn't want Tea Cake and wanted him dead, then that was a real sin and a shame." She is not misunderstood. Finally, Janie's voice is effective in the outside world, as it had been within her relationship with Tea Cake. Janie articulates their love to the external world as Tea Cake had "articulated" it, made it understood, in slapping Janie.

Janie's Hard Won Authority

Chapter 20, like Chapter 10, functions as a transition between the Everglades and Eatonville—from phase two to the beginning and end of phase three, which is Janie's narration of phases one and two. Again, the separating dots appear, indicating a phase-shift. But instead of introducing a component phase, the dots here preface a broad phase within which the other two major phases exist.

As Janie tells her story to Pheoby, she establishes a past that belongs to her, is her possession. But Janie's past is nothing but herself, so that her voice articulates herself—the self that now belongs to itself. And this new self-possession grants Janie authority in her own right, in her past's right. She no longer needs authorization to speak effectively.

Nevertheless, Zora Neale Hurston does authorize both Janie and her voice. By Hurston's writing down, author(iz)ing, Janie's life, Janie's entire past becomes present—not just her past at a specific point in her narration. Time no longer limits Janie. She will live forever in the continual self-authorizing present of *Their Eyes Were Watching God.* Her dreams will not "be mocked to death by Time."

Hurston Must Reject Romance to Fulfill Janie's Quest

Brenda R. Smith

Brenda R. Smith is an assistant professor of English at Kent State University–Stark in Ohio, where she teaches African American literature, Women's literature, and American literature.

In this viewpoint, Smith places Janie's story within the tradition of the bildungsroman, a German term for a novel of education, in the sense of the moral and psychological growth of the protagonist, usually in the context of a quest or journey. Their Eyes Were Watching God *combines two types of novel, Smith asserts, the novel of education and the romance. Through organic metaphors, Hurston reinforces the naturalness of Janie's quest, Smith writes. But in order for Janie to fulfill her* Bildung, *or education, Hurston must reject the other half of the story, the romance. Thus it is that Hurston kills off Tea Cake and leaves Janie to reconstruct her life to Pheoby at the end of the novel in order to achieve full self-awareness.*

Zora Neale Hurston's protagonist, Janie Crawford, in *Their Eyes Were Watching God* is, according to [critic] Eva Boesenberg, "the first fictional Black female quester in her own right, a female protagonist whose maturation involves intimate relationships with men, but is not restricted to them. . . . [Janie's story is] a quest for full personal growth [Bildung] superimposed on a romantic plot." The romance and quest plots are intertwined throughout the novel; Hurston, as author, and Janie, as narrator-protagonist, must each reconcile this dialectical tension in order to "reap" a successful *Bildung* for Janie.

Brenda R. Smith, *New Essays on the African American Novel: From Hurston and Ellison to Morrison and Whitehead*, ed. Lovalerie King and Linda F. Selzer. Palgrave Macmillan, 2008, pp. 125–29. © Lovalerie King and Linda F. Selzer, 2008. Reproduced with permission of Palgrave Macmillan.

Hurston's novel arguably can be divided into three major sections, paralleling the stages of the traditional female hero quest paradigm: (i) The Call to Quest; (ii) The Journey; and (iii) The Return; each section of Hurston's novel represents a different stage of Janie's quest toward selfhood. However, Hurston adapts and transforms the conventions of the traditional paradigm, integrating these stages with narrative strategies that situate the text within a female *Bildung* tradition that is identifiably African American.

An Organic Quest

One of Hurston's most significant narrative strategies is her use of organic imagery to structure her text. . . . By positing Janie's *Bildung* as "organic," Hurston transcends the limiting social conventions and prescribed social roles for black women during the period and imbues Janie's *Bildung* with a "piety" and "purity" that facilitates Hurston's writing her protagonist into the romance paradigm.

An equally significant strategy that situates Hurston's text within the black female *Bildungsroman* [novel of personal growth] tradition is the later beginning of *Bildung* that is characteristic for black female protagonists. As the novel begins, Janie's *Bildung* is completed, and she returns to Eatonville to narrate to her friend, Pheoby Watson, the text of her journey to selfhood. Janie begins by telling Pheoby that "her conscious life" had begun at the age of sixteen, when she lay under "a blossoming pear tree" in her back yard and watched a bee pollinate a bloom. She identifies with the pear tree; as she leans over the gate post "waiting for the world to be made," she commits herself to finding "a bee to her bloom". From this, it is clear that Hurston combines romantic love (the pear tree) and quest (the world) from the beginning of the novel. At this point in the narrative, Hurston also constructs an inside/outside dichotomy, which is characteristic of female *Bildungsroman*. Such a dichotomy reflects the reality that although the female protagonist's *Bildung* may involve a physical journey, it typically begins, and may persist, as a psychological, or internal, one. Although the seeds of quest have been sown in Janie's psyche, she is "gated in," and her journey to the horizon is deferred.

The pear tree vision is also compromised or indefinitely deferred by Janie's grandmother Nanny, who, as a former slave and the female ancestral figure in the narrative, embodies society's notions of black womanhood. Recalling her and her daughter Leafy's experiences of rape in slavery and freedom, respectively, Nanny testifies to the experiences of racial and sexual oppression that have left her with the belief that the black woman "is de mule of the world." When Nanny witnesses Janie kissing a neighbor boy over the front gate, she imposes her text of black womanhood onto Janie, declaring Janie a sexual being—a woman. Consequently, there is only one way for her to avoid being exploited by "de menfolks white or Black": She must marry a man who can provide her material stability, respectability, and "protection"; and Nanny has chosen Logan Killicks, a widower who has "sixty acres uh land right on de big road." Janie sacrifices her vision to Nanny's and hopes that marriage to Killicks will bring romantic love.

Inside Versus Outside

Janie's marriage to Logan Killicks and her marriage to Joe Stark, for whom she leaves Killicks, comprise the first and second stages, respectively, of Janie's *Bildung*. In form, Janie's marriage to Killicks fulfills her vision of marriage. In fact, however, Janie's marriage comes without the intensity of emotion and reciprocity that satisfies her pear tree vision. Living in isolation from the larger community, with a husband who ultimately tries to turn her into the "mule" Nanny sought to prevent her from becoming, Janie quickly realizes that marriage does not guarantee love. With this realization, Janie's "first dream was dead."

Janie's marriage to Joe Starks, "a citified, stylishly dressed man" on his way to Eatonville, Florida, to "be a big voice" foregrounds the quest plot. Starks is the "vehicle" by which Janie embarks on her physical journey. Although Starks, like Killicks, "[does] not represent sun-up and pollen and blooming trees," he does speak "for far horizon . . . for change and chance." However, Starks ultimately subverts both Janie's vision of the blossoming pear tree and the promise of the horizon. He "forbids [Janie] to indulge" in the daily store porch conversations with the other townsfolk and excludes her from participation in the town's rituals and traditions. Consequently, Janie comes to realize that she has "no more blossomy openings dusting pollen over her man."

The inside/outside dichotomy persists as Janie's "outside" continues to "go . . . about . . . prostrating itself before Jody," while her "inside" sticks "out into the future, imagining her life different from what it was." However, rather than a physical movement outward, the dichotomy in this instance heralds Janie's coming to voice. Janie's bitterness and resentment at having to, again, sacrifice her pear tree vision spills over into a very public confrontation with Joe when he personally insults her in front of the men folk of the town for making a mistake in the store. Janie, for the first time ever, squares off with Joe and says: "Naw, Ah ain't no young gal no mo' . . . But Ah'm uh woman every inch of me. Talkin' 'bout *me* lookin' old! When you pull down yo' britches, you look lak de change uh life." In coming to voice, Janie affirms her femaleness—the first step in her self-actualization—frees herself from the oppression she has experienced in her marriage, and effectively strips Joe of his masculinity. As a result, she and Joe are permanently estranged; and Joe's health drastically declines, resulting in his death.

With Janie's third marriage to Vergible "Tea Cake" Woods, Hurston realizes the telos [goal] of her romance plot. Janie and Tea Cake's union is, for Janie, a reciprocal relationship that satisfies her vision of "organic union." She and Tea Cake are coworkers and peers. Tea Cake also speaks for horizon. He takes Janie to the muck, the Florida Everglades, where Janie becomes an accepted member of and a participant in the African American community. She can tell the stories she longed to share with the townsfolk when she was married to Joe. The narrative, at this point, indicates the culmination of the love/quest dialectic. . . . Although Tea Cake facilitates Janie's coming into communion with the world, he problematizes the quest plot. With Tea Cake, Janie reaps the benefits of *Bildung* without actual quest. Her status in the community is predicated on her position as Tea Cake's wife. Also, Janie's love for Tea Cake is described as "self-crushing"; she seems satisfied to cede her autonomy and independence in favor of the pear tree vision.

Moving Beyond Romance

If Hurston is to reap a successful *Bildung* from the seeds of quest she has sown, she must move Janie beyond a love that threatens her sense of self and resume Janie's quest. In order to reposition the narrative within the *Bildung* paradigm, Hurston reverts to what Boesenberg terms an "antiquated solution to the female [hero's] dilemma . . . the death of the male partner." Hurston effects Tea Cake's demise; and, in order to privilege the restoration of Janie's agency, she uses her protagonist to assist her. A hurricane unleashes its violence on the muck, and Tea Cake is bitten by a rabid dog as he and Janie try to make their way to safety. Tea Cake subsequently contracts rabies; and when he, in a rabies-induced fit of jealousy, attempts to shoot Janie, she grabs a rifle and kills him in self-defense. In both female and male *Bildungsroman* paradigms, the protagonists, in order to achieve full self-awareness, must confront and reconcile themselves to their mortality—and they must ultimately affirm life. Janie does this when she chooses her life over Tea Cake's. Hurston mitigates Janie's culpability in Tea Cake's death and preserves the idyll of Janie and Tea Cake's union by using the master paradigm of "God as Nature," an elaboration on her use of organic imagery in the text. By representing Tea Cake's death as the inevitable and uncontrollable culmination of a series of events . . . Hurston is able to preserve Janie's romantic vision even as she reaffirms her autonomy and agency.

Ultimately, however, Janie's successful *Bildung* has been achieved at the expense of romance. When Janie returns to Eatonville, Hurston must rely on Janie's recreation of the romance plot in her text of self in order for romance and quest to coexist and be integrated at the resolution of the novel. While memories of Tea Cake "[make] pictures of love and light against the wall", Janie is, in fact, alone. Only the telos of the horizon persists: "[Janie] pulled in her horizon like a great fish-net . . . and draped it over her shoulder." Although, as Boesenberg states, "Hurston writes beyond the ending decreed for heroines in the conventional romance plot, marriage or death, [in that] Janie chooses her life over both marriage *and* death." Hurston's appropriation of the romance paradigm ultimately limits the strategies she has at her use to resolve the dialectic between love and quest that exists in her text.

Janie Crawford's Quest Ends in Death

Darryl Hattenhauer

Darryl Hattenhauer teaches at Arizona State University. He is the author of Shirley Jackson's American Gothic.

Hattenhauer suggests in the following viewpoint that Hurston was always a complicated and contradictory writer. The ending of Their Eyes Were Watching God *affirms these traits by implying that Janie's quest will end tragically: she will die from rabies, contracted when Tea Cake bites her arm during his own death scene. Hattenhauer believes that Janie is even more obsessed than Nanny with living out the American Dream modeled by the dominant white culture. In chasing this horizon, Hattenhauer maintains, Janie denies her impending death, stays eternally an adolescent, and affirms the values of white America. Hurston has thus written a complicated study of a woman whose quest for love and acceptance kills her.*

In her tribute to Zora Neale Hurston, [American novelist] Alice Walker acknowledges that Hurston could sometimes be paradoxical. For example, her feminism and her ethnic pride seem not to correspond with her conservative politics. Not surprisingly, then, Hurston's autobiography, *Dust Tracks on a Road*, has long been recognized as sometimes contradictory and often evasive. [Her biographer] Robert E. Hemenway notes that "style in *Dust Tracks* becomes a kind of camouflage, an escape from articulating the paradoxes of her personality." But it is not just her life and her narrative about it that are contradictory. Of her prose in general, [critic] Henry Louis Gates says that "hers is a rhetoric of division." And of *Their*

Darryl Hattenhauer, "The Death of Janie Crawford: Tragedy and the American Dream in 'Their Eyes Were Watching God'," *MELUS*, vol. 19, 1994. Reproduced by permission.

Eyes Were Watching God in particular, he characterizes the narration as "a divided voice, a double voice unreconciled."

Subverting the Text

Similarly, recent scholarship on *Their Eyes* finds that this complex narrative is underlain by a subtext that subverts the surface text. [Critic] Susan Willis argues that despite the text's apparent affirmation of black life, Hurston overlooks the realities of class:

> She chooses not to depict the northern migration of black people, which brought Hurston herself to New York and a college degree and brought thousands of other rural blacks to the metropolis and wage labor. In this, Hurston sets a precedent in black women's writing that will leave unexplored the possibility of a black working-class culture in this country.

More specifically, Willis finds that Hurston's treatment of farm labor minimizes the effects of exploitation:

> Janie and Tea Cake are really not inscribed within the economics of the "muck." If they plant and harvest beans, they do so because they enjoy fieldwork and because it allows them to live in the heart of southern black cultural production. They are not, like many of the other migrant workers, bowed down by debts and kids. . . . Janie, with a large inheritance in the bank, need not work at all and Tea Cake, whose forte is gambling, need never accept a job unless he wants it.

Similarly, [critic] Jennifer Jordan argues that Janie, who is married to Eatonville's mayor and chief property owner, is a privileged bourgeois. For some, Janie even bears comparison with the canonical characters of the dominant culture's literary tradition, those . . . who leave home and venture into space. [Critic] Michael Awkward, for example, notes that Janie "envisions herself as Adam—a signal creation without a mate" and outside of history. And [critic] James Krasner finds that

"Janie's life story is built on the male model." It seems fitting, then, that in her autobiography Hurston takes pride in her patrimony: "The village of Eatonville is still governed by the laws formulated by my father." To these new departures in Hurston criticism, I will add that Janie is dying in the end, that she denies her impending death, that she is an eternal adolescent, that it is Janie more than Nanny who affirms the values of the dominant culture, and that Hurston has written a complex and ironic study of the psychology of denial.

Janie's Death Foreshadowed

As the literally rabid Tea Cake dies, he bites Janie on the arm. And he does it so severely that she has to pry his teeth out of her flesh. Yet there is no explicit statement to indicate whether or not Janie gets anti-rabies shots. Either Hurston was so lacking in narrative ability that she suggested her protagonist's infection with rabies and then failed to resolve the situation, or Hurston made the resolution implicit. Several foreshadowings suggest the latter. The announcement of Tea Cake's death in the beginning (the first chapter in this flashback plot includes some events from the end of the story) imparts the fated quality of tragedy. In the beginning, Janie is returning from Tea Cake's death, and she conceives of her life as "a great tree in leaf with the things suffered." She thinks of the tree as something that contains not only birth and growth but also decline and death: "Dawn and doom was in the branches." Her death, which was implicit in her budding youth (because death is always implicit in the life cycle), is explicit in the branching off of her adult quest for love and freedom. Just as the narrator foreshadows Janie's death in the beginning of the text and in the beginning of Janie's life, the narrator suggests more specifically in the final pages that Janie's death is an outgrowth of her adolescence. The symbol of the mature leafy tree grows out of the symbol of the pear tree that the sixteen-year-old Janie expresses as a metaphor for her emerging sexuality. Not until the end of the novel does she see that death, not just sexuality, is implicit in nature. The growing tree, then, symbolizes both Janie's life as well as the narrator's plot.

That Janie will probably die is also foreshadowed when she and Pheoby discuss Janie's burgeoning romance with Tea Cake. Pheoby compares Janie to Annie Tyler, another wealthy middle-aged woman who took up with a younger man, but only to have him steal her money and leave her heart as empty as her pockets: "She had waited all her life for something, and it killed her when it found her." And during the hurricane, when it appears that Janie and Tea Cake will drown, Tea Cake asks her if she regrets having gone with him, and she assures him that an early death would be a small price to pay for the prize of having Tea Cake's love for two years: "If you can see de light at daybreak, you don't keer if you die at dusk." In addition, there is the dramatic irony of Janie thinking to herself that the dog which mortally wounded Tea Cake has (by taking her man) metaphorically killed her too: "That big old dawg . . . had killed her after all." But more foreshadowing reveals that soon her death will probably be no longer just a metaphor. Doctor Simmons warns her that Tea Cake is "liable to bite somebody else, specially you, and then you'll be in the same fix he's in." Moreover, Doctor Simmons testifies in court that "he found Janie all bit in the arm. . . ." And after Tea Cake's death, she tries to accept not only his passing but her own by imagining their reunion in heaven. The narrator, who often uses free indirect speech to paraphrase Janie's thoughts, states: "He would be thinking up new songs to play her when she got there." The narrator also foreshadows the shooting of Tea Cake with the dramatic irony not only of his teaching Janie how to shoot, but also of his saying that there is "always some trashy rascal that needs a good killin.'"

Darryl Hattenhauer thinks that critics who read Their Eyes Were Watching God *as a triumph for Janie have overlooked the fact that she will die tragically in the end because, though she had already fired the shot that would kill Tea Cake, he passed on the rabies by biting her as he died.* © Gabe Palmer/Alamy.

Undercutting Romantic Love

Janie seems to be motivated partly out of unconscious self-destructiveness. First, she could have run away. In free indirect speech again, the narrator tells us that when Janie finds that Tea Cake has hidden a pistol, she realizes that flight is one of her options: "She could either run or try to take it away before it was too late." Then she refuses to put Tea Cake in the hospital where he would be no danger to her. Next, she does not flee when she discovers the loaded revolver under his pillow. And finally, she does not unload his revolver, but instead turns the cylinder (which has three rounds in it) so that he will have to pull the trigger three times before it will shoot (the hammer will fall on an empty cylinder each of the first three times). This strategy is very risky because he might break open the revolver and discover that the cylinder has been rotated, which might in turn make him violent immediately. Accomplished with firearms, Janie knows that if he checks the cylinder, all he has to do is turn it so that it will fire the first three times he pulls the trigger. Janie, then, appears to be so overwrought both at the probable death of Tea Cake and at her own possible demise that she denies the existence of both of these tragic possibilities (thereby helping to ensure that both will come to pass). Her conscious mind resists fate insofar as she denies Tea Cake's death while nonetheless trying to arrange things so that she might die with him.

She could also be denying his hostility towards her. While she arranges the guns, she denies the need to flee: "Tea Cake wouldn't hurt her. He was just jealous and wanted to scare her." And she tells herself that they will "laugh over it when he [gets] well." Even when he points the pistol at her, she denies the threat: "Maybe he would point to scare her, that was all." But recently Tea Cake has not only beaten her, but done so not because of any wrongdoing of hers but simply to show their acquaintances that he controls her.

This repeated denial points not only to certain character traits but also to previously overlooked themes. It is the cruelest of ironies that each has to die for loving the other. Thus the text undercuts its thematic veneer of romantic love. . . . Tea Cake bites Janie to take her with him. Just as the symbols of nature reveal the mind of the protagonist and the tragic quality of the plot, they also suggest more about the novel's theme. For just as the symbol of the tree presides over Janie's youth and death, the symbol of the horizon begins and ends the narrative. The narrator's meditation on the horizon at the start of the novel makes the romantic assertion not only that women are immune to the ravages of time but also that they achieve such immunity by denial—by blocking out unpleasant reality—and substituting dreams for it:

> Ships at a distance have every man's wish on board. For some they come in with the tide. For others they sail forever on the horizon, never out of sight, never landing until the Watcher turns his eyes away in resignation, his dreams mocked to death by Time. That is the life of men. Now, women forget all those things they don't want to remember, and remember everything they don't want to forget. The dream is the truth. Then they act and do things accordingly. So the beginning of this was a woman and she had come back from burying the dead.

Moreover, at the end, Janie says she's "been tuh de horizon," and she elsewhere identifies Tea Cake with the horizon: he is "the son of Evening Sun." Furthermore, in an ironic close to the scene in which the white women comfort Janie for ostensibly having to shoot Tea Cake, the narrator states, "So the sun went down." Thus Tea Cake is born of the horizon; he is a kind of avatar of nature whom Janie hopes is a pollen bearing bee. In the final scene as she stares out at the dark horizon (which recalls her statement about dying at dusk), she is overtaken by a vision of Tea Cake "with the sun for a shawl." Then come the last lines of the novel:

> Here was peace. She pulled in her horizon like a great fish-
> net. Pulled it from around the waist of the world and draped
> it over her shoulder. So much of life in its meshes! She
> called in her soul to come and see.

Here Tea Cake and the horizon are merged in the image of
the shawl-like net, and she harvests them and drapes them
over her shoulder in a Christian death image. But her revery
is mocked to death by Time. She hasn't avoided the ravages of
Time by denying death; she has not realized her dream by es-
caping into metaphors of nature. The pear tree has turned
into the leafy "doom," and her fish-net horizon has yielded the
dead body of her life's one great catch. Denying what she does
not want to remember has not allowed her to realize her fantasy of romance and unfettered individuation. Her version of
the American dream is not the truth.

The merging of the horizon with the image of Tea Cake in
a shawl suggests a further ironic complication. It is remark-
able for Janie to imagine Tea Cake wearing a shawl, which is a
garment that she would more readily associate with an old
woman. More specifically, it suggests Nanny. In Janie's final vision of nature, then, the pear tree has gone leafy, and her image of Tea Cake fuses with both the horizon and Nanny, which
suggests the complex origins of Janie's values, attitudes, and
aspirations. After Jody's death, Janie asserts that she has always
hated Nanny for trying to make her live like whites. As we will
see, Janie's charge is partially valid, for Nanny has spent much
of her life with whites and passed along some of their traits to
Janie. But we must distinguish between which of Nanny's values Janie maintains and which of Nanny's values Janie does
not. For if aspects of African culture survive in Afro-American
culture, certainly aspects of the dominant culture are present
in Afro-American culture as well. . . .

Janie is greatly influenced by white America. . . . She is
raised with whites in an environment where not only the
whites but also the blacks (with their high value on light skin,

straight hair, etc.) affirm white standards. Yet before the white jury frees her, she fears the white jury as alien: "What need had they to leave their richness to come look on Janie in her overalls?" But Janie is richer than many of the whites: she has inherited Jody's home and store, and she collects rents on his real estate holdings. And after the verdict of innocent, Janie regards them as "the kind white friends who had realized her feelings." No wonder Killicks tells her, "You think youse white folks by de way you act." . . . Where the whites continually prate about the eyes of the world watching as they carry the shining beacon of sacred self-interest on their mission into the new promised land, Janie imagines herself and her errand in similar terms:

> She had been getting ready for her great journey to the ho-
> rizons in search of people; it was important to all the world
> that she would find them and they find her. . . . She had
> found a jewel down inside herself and she had wanted to
> walk where people could see her and gleam it around. . . .

White Culture's Influence

The white dominant culture's influence on Janie has further implications. When Janie tells herself just after Jody dies that she has hated Nanny all her life, the narrator notes: "She hated her grandmother and had hidden it from herself all these years under a cloak of pity." While Janie maintains her illusion of freedom by denying that Nanny still influences her, Janie pretends that she is just as free of Jody. The narrator shows that in Janie's mind Nanny constricted the horizon and choked Janie with it: "Nanny had taken the . . . horizon . . . and pinched it in to such a little bit of a thing that she could tie it about her granddaughter's neck tight enough to choke her." But the end of the story does not validate Janie's impulse for freedom. Rather, it merges Tea Cake and Nanny with the horizon image: Tea Cake becomes part of the horizon that chokes her. Indeed, victims of hydrophobia [rabies] suffer from a constriction of the neck and throat muscles.

Similarly, her hopes for her relationship with Jody also suggest this deterministic view of the tragic impossibility of Janie's quest. Janie ' agrees to go with Jody because he speaks "for far horizon." And when this Adamic heroine walks down the road to join Jody, she is overcome by "a feeling of sudden newness and change. . . ." This image of rebirth through departure also appears when she is on the road and "waiting for the world to be made." Her penchant for the mobility of the American dream contrasts with what Nanny would have her do. In alleging her hatred for Nanny, Janie correctly assumes that leaving Killicks for Jody is inconsistent with Nanny's wishes, but it violates only Nanny's wish that Janie marry Killicks; it affirms Nanny's advice that Janie have a dream and follow it. Janie says, "Ah done lived Grandma's way, now Ah means tuh live mine." But living her own life in a way Nanny would not have wanted becomes her desire largely because Nanny gave her the value of following her "wish." Thus Janie unwittingly affirms what her elders taught her even as she negates it. . . . She now tries to blame Nanny for the twenty years of brow beating under Jody, but it was Janie's own desire to run away with him. It is no longer the farm but the city that informs the American dream, and Nanny wants Janie to avoid the white folks's yard by going to a black man's farm. It is Janie who decides to stay in the new version of the white folks's yard, Jody's white house.

The white influence on Janie makes her feel and act superior. As we have seen, Killicks tells her that she acts like white people. And when Janie returns after losing Tea Cake, she walks right past Pheoby and her friends, clearly snubbing them. Minutes later Pheoby goes to her and says, "You always did class off." Janie denies it by saying, "Jody classed me off. Ah didn't." Yet when Jody tells her that she will be "the bell-cow" superior to the other women in the town Janie does not object. . . .

Janie exhibits the dominant culture's belief that there are no borders on human aspiration—that one can be whatever one wants to be, that one can have it all. After she inherits Jody's wealth, she rejoices that she will "have the rest of her life to do as she please[s]" rather than the rest of her life to do what she should. For the dominant culture declares that there is no difference.

Living and Dying in Denial

In the end, Janie is at least partly aware of her fall. She says she is going to make "comparisons" and her image of the budding tree gone leafy implicitly suggests her likeness to her tragically fallen mother, who was called "Leafy." She might also compare herself to what she would have become had she stayed with Killicks: a wealthy widow. She might also compare herself to what she might have become if she had run off with Johnny Taylor: a bigot like Mrs. Turner, or a beggar like Mrs. Tony, or the dying widow that she is (for shiftless Johnny Taylor is akin to shiftless Tea Cake). She might even realize that old Killicks feared the faithlessness of his young lover just as Janie feared the faithlessness of hers. As she symbolically grooms herself for death by combing the road dust out of her hair and washing it from her feet, she laughs a little, perhaps realizing how much she has come to compare with Killicks and his stinky feet, which she wanted him to wash before he lay himself down to sleep. And perhaps she laughs too at the irony of washing her feet when she will soon, like Tea Cake, suffer the ravages of hydrophobia.

She might also recall her statement that "it's so many people never see de light at all" and be thankful that, as she conceives of it, she sees the light at last: her fate is to wait and see if God's will is to take her life. When Tea Cake, Motor Boat and Janie seek shelter from the hurricane, they are enclosed in darkness: "They seemed to be staring at the dark, but their eyes were watching God." Janie says, "Ole Massa is doin' His work now. Us oughta keep quiet." Soon Tea Cake will ask of the dog that bites him, "Wonder where he came from?. . ." Similarly, Janie questions God when she learns that Tea Cake has rabies; she looks to the sky for some sign, some answer as to whether Tea Cake will live. On the next page, the answer comes from Doc: no serum is available; they will have to wait for it to come from Miami. When Janie says that it is too cruel "to kill her through Tea Cake," she implies that the agent of the action is God, acting through nature. Thus she regards the rabies as God's will. God has freed Motor Boat from seemingly certain death, and yet He has inflicted Tea Cake with rabies. And by trying to deny Tea Cake's fate—in trying to deny what she regards as God's will—she has contracted rabies. But by waiting to see if God's will is that she die and thereby rejoin Tea Cake, she accepts her fate even as she denies it—denies it to herself and to her audience, Pheoby and the townsfolk. That is what she means when she tells Pheoby that all people "got tuh go tuh God."

After listening to Janie's story of the quest, Pheoby says that she is not satisfied with her life anymore and adds that the solution is to get her husband to take her fishing. It was after a fishing excursion that Janie fell in love with Tea Cake. Thus Janie, a tragic heroine whose journey has been even more psychological than geographic, realizes that she cannot explain to Pheoby the complexity of her journey: "Pheoby, you got to go there to know there." She repeats this idea when she tells Pheoby that people "got tuh find out about livin' fuh theyselves." And they also have to find out about dying— about the "doom" implicit in nature and life. And this tragic truth, Janie has learned, is something no one could have told her, and something she cannot tell anyone. Thus Janie is not the narrator for two reasons: she cannot admit the truth, and she will no longer be alive to tell it.

Social Issues in Literature

CHAPTER 3

Contemporary Perspectives on Women's Issues

Women Do Not Need to Be Like Men to Be Successful

Kathleen Parker

Kathleen Parker is a nationally syndicated columnist who writes for the Washington Post. *She won the 2010 Pulitzer Prize for Commentary.*

In this viewpoint Parker writes that for a long time she has found fault with feminists and their causes; however, during a recent trip to the United Arab Emirates her observations and discussions with women of that country have reinvigorated her sense of feminism. For too long, Parker writes, women have tried to gain equality with males by attempting to emulate men. This is the wrong tactic, she believes. There are some things that men are better at, and some things that women excel in, she asserts, and the difference between the sexes must be acknowledged; nevertheless, women should become more active in leadership roles and strive for feminine heroism.

Among life's surreal experiences, few can compare with finding myself seated on a baroque bench, one of dozens lining the perimeter of an ornate drawing room in the palace of Sheikha Fatima Bint Mubarak [wife of the late president of the United Arab Emirates, or U.A.E.] in [the emirate of] Abu Dhabi, chatting it up with three Ph.D.-endowed women sheathed in black abayas, sipping sweet hot tea and eating candies. "I think you Americans do not enjoy being women as much as we do," said one, peering into my face with an earnestness one usually associates with grim news delivered to next of kin.

Say what?

Born-Again Feminist

Pressed further, she allowed that American women, in their quest for equality with men, had surrendered some of their uniquely feminine traits and attendant pleasures. The occasion was a luncheon in honor of then-first lady Laura Bush given by Sheikha Fatima, widow of the founder of the United Arab Emirates, on the first stop of a four-country tour to launch a partnership to fight breast cancer. From the U.A.E. we traveled to Kuwait, where we met courageous women who, having just been granted the vote the year before, had recently run for public office. None won, but they ran.

It was an inspiring trip, as one might imagine. For me personally, having just turned in the manuscript for my book *Save the Males*, it was life-altering. Not to be rash, but I dare say I've become a born-again feminist after decades of feeling that feminism had veered off course. When the National Organization for Women turned out to protest golf-club memberships, I figured it was time to alphabetize the CDs. All done here.

I stand by my book's argument that males need to be saved to the extent that, too often, equality has become a zero-sum game in which girls' success has meant shortchanging boys. Like my friends in Abu Dhabi, I believe that American women have paid dearly for the privilege of having a voice in the conduct of their lives. Have they failed to enjoy being women? To each her own determination, but I would submit that in trying to find a place in a male-ordered world, women have paid more than their fair dues, much to the detriment of their mental health and their families.

But meeting women of the Middle East—breaking bread with them, seeing beyond the clouds of fabric, bearing witness to suffrage on the ground floor and the courage required for women to sally forth—combined to awaken something long dormant. Perhaps it is a matter of stakes and battles worth

This photograph was taken at the luncheon mentioned by writer Kathleen Parker—a luncheon attended by former First Lady Laura Bush and hosted by Sheikha Fatima Bin Mubarak on October 22, 2007, in Abu Dhabi, United Arab Emirates. © Shealah Craighead/AP Images.

fighting. The struggle for free expression in cultures that condone sacrificing women to men's honor gets the blood pumping again.

Feminism Has Grown Stale

I've been fortunate to meet some of the women included in this magazine [*Newsweek*] and have been mesmerized by their intelligence, grace, and courage. While we Westerners have never had to contend with a Taliban or a theocratic state that treats women as subhuman, we are reminded that the rights we take for granted are not exactly growing mold.

Nevertheless, the feminism of my youth did grow stale and, over time, often became silly. Or so it seemed to me and, apparently, to many other women who became mothers and workers and knew that the real world of juggling career and family wasn't a calling but a curse. We were trying not just to be as good as men, but to be men. I have the neckties to prove it. It turns out that women make lousy men, a fact for which we should feel grateful rather than apologetic. As a group, we are worse at some things, but better at others—the very "others," it also turns out, that happen to be driving today's economy and that of the future.

Consequently, in the U.S. today, women hold a majority of the jobs, and dominate in colleges and professional schools. They also hold a majority of managerial and professional positions, and about half of all accounting, banking, and insurance jobs.

These socioeconomic facts don't mean that women have achieved perfect parity with men, who still dominate at the highest levels of business. As Hanna Rosin reported in *The Atlantic*, men are more assertive in the job market, tending, for example, to negotiate the terms of their first jobs out of college (57 percent, compared with only 7 percent of women). Men are also more self-assured and, perhaps relatedly, hold most upper-management positions. Only 3 percent of the Fortune 500 CEOs are women. In Britain, debate has recently centered on the paucity of women in corporate-board positions and whether this gap should be addressed through quotas. Former trade minister Mervyn Davies says U.K.-listed companies in the FTSE 100 [top British Companies] should have 25 percent female board membership by 2015. For now, owing largely to objections from accomplished women who feel patronized by the suggestion of quotas, companies will be left to meet the new standard voluntarily.

The most glaring lack of female participation is also the most ironic. Here in the U.S., the longest-running democracy on the planet, relatively few women hold legislative positions. Even though more women than ever ran in the recent [2010] midterm elections, fewer are serving now than in the previous Congress. Women hold only 17 seats in the 100-seat Senate and just 75 (roughly 16 percent) in the House of Representatives. Many developing countries, including Iraq and Afghanistan, can boast far greater legislative participation by women. Three Kazakh women have so far applied for candidacy in the country's April 3 presidential election. In Liberia a woman is president.

Women Can Achieve Heroism

Why are women lagging in this of all countries? It may be a matter of round pegs and square holes. Women have tried to fit into a male-constructed world and found it either uninviting or inflexible to their needs. They don't make it to the top of corporations because they find the long hours and travel impossible to manage with children at home. Too, they may find themselves alienated by masculine style, which psychologists Alice Eagly and Linda Carli describe as controlling, versus women's, which tends to take into greater consideration the rights of others.

The confounding factors are many, surely. But what we enlightened Westerners know is that empowering women empowers us all. Research shows that companies with more female employees make more money. And recent history makes clear that nations that oppress women are dangerous nations. Until women are equal partners in the human race, we are less secure and surely less interesting.

A year or so ago, I was asked to speak to the women's legislative caucus in South Carolina, the state with the fewest number of women serving in public office. I was asked to say something inspiring to encourage them to enter politics. I finally settled on lessons learned in the Middle East.

Women should run for public office, I told them, because—they can. Because other women around the world are watching to see how it's done. And because we are quite simply their role models—and their hope.

When women achieve parity in boardrooms and legislatures, they'll no longer have to twist into male versions of themselves but can help fashion a world that is a better fit for them and the human beings they create. You won't find me pushing for a Swedish model, in which "velvet dads" [who take parental leave from jobs] are penalized for not staying home with Baby. But somewhere between the abayas of Abu Dhabi and the pistol-packin', "man-up" mamas of Wingnut, America, is a strong, compassionate, heroic womanhood of which we can all feel a part and be proud sisters. And brothers, too.

Domestic Violence Is Disproportionately High Among African Americans

Marie Tessier

Marie Tessier is a writer who covers national, international, and financial affairs, with a particular expertise in violence against women. Her work has appeared in Ms. magazine, in the Columbia Journalism Review, on National Public Radio, and in newspapers throughout the country.

Tessier reports here that the incidence of domestic violence in the African American community is disproportionately high. African American women are twice as likely as white women to die at the hands of a significant other. While many believe that poverty shapes statistics regarding domestic violence, those with higher incomes are not immune. One of the impediments to dealing with African American domestic violence is that those in the black community do not always trust the police or social service agencies. Therefore, victims may be reluctant to involve the authorities in domestic matters, Tessier suggests.

Activists in the growing movement to support battered African-American women agree on what's needed to stem domestic violence: more services that are culturally informed and integrated into victims' communities.

A Higher Risk

"Color blindness is not what you need if you're trying to serve diverse communities," says Oliver Williams, executive director of the Institute on Domestic Violence in the African-American

Marie Tessier, "Domestic Violence among African Americans: Domestic Violence, Is It a Black Thing?," *The District Chronicles*, 2007. Reproduced by permission.

Community at the University of Minnesota in Minneapolis. "The trend is toward an increase in community-based, faith-based, and grassroots services."

While the battered women's movement has long striven to serve all women, few projects can identify specific programs designed to reach out to diverse communities. That can be a barrier to safety for black women, who tend to reach out for help through informal networks in their communities, such as a church, rather than consulting a shelter or hotline, according to experts.

African-American women face a higher risk for experiencing domestic violence than other women, according to the most recent data from the Justice Department. In fact, they are more than twice as likely to die at the hands of a spouse or a boyfriend. They are also at greater risk of more severe violence, according to the Centers for Disease Control in Atlanta and the Bureau of Justice Statistics (BJS) in Washington, DC.

"When you're talking about African-American women, you're talking about everything bad about family violence, and then some," says Tonya Lovelace, executive director of the Women of Color Network, a project of the National Resource Center on Domestic Violence based in Harrisburg, Pennsylvania. "The way that communities of color experience violence is affected by our history, and by other issues." Some behavior can be grouped by race, but differences can be deceiving, Williams said.

"Black women are more likely to leave than other women, but they are also more likely to return," he said. "A lot of the reasons may speak more to poverty and a lack of resources, because a woman may just not have a different place to go."

Organizations such as Atlanta's Black Church and Domestic Violence Institute, Williams' institute, and the National Resource Center on Domestic Violence's Women of Color Network are all engaged in training domestic violence groups and community service agencies in each others' work.

Much of the funding comes through the federal Violence Against Women Act, and much of the activity is coordinated and supported by the Violence Against Women Office at the U.S. Department of Justice. National groups such as the National Network to End Domestic Violence in Washington, DC, and the National Resource Center on Domestic Violence coordinate and facilitate the work.

While scholars and activists agree that higher rates of poverty among African-Americans probably shape some statistics about violence, they are quick to point out that higher incomes do not immunize against domestic violence.

A Higher Rate of Homicide

An October 2006 article in *Essence* magazine, for example, details how Prince George's County, Maryland, the wealthiest predominantly black county in the nation, has a high rate of intimate partner homicide. According to the Maryland Network Against Domestic Violence, 48 people, mostly women, died there between 2001 and 2006 as a result of domestic violence, second only to Baltimore County which had 72 deaths.

One of the starkest realities for African-American women is their vulnerability to homicide. The risk of violence is higher for women in bigger cities, according to the BJS.

Homicide is the second leading cause of death for black women between the ages of 15 and 24, according to the Centers for Disease Control. Only young black men have a higher homicide rate, and only black men have a higher rate of intimate partner homicide than black women, BJS reported.

Barriers to seeking help are believed to contribute to the higher rate of homicide for both women and men because violence has escalated to a greater degree before a woman can reach safety, scholars and activists generally agree. The homicide rate for black men has dropped more than for black women in recent decades, according to federal statistics.

All the factors that contribute to greater violence probably explain the higher intimate partner homicide rate of black men, Lovelace said. "Black women get arrested more, we get convicted more, and we have had fewer places to go. The statistics don't account for self-defense," she said.

Roadblocks to Safety

One of the biggest roadblocks to safety, says Tricia Bent-Goodley, a professor at Howard University, is the troubled, violent histories many black communities have with the police and social service agencies. That provides one more cultural barrier to seeking police intervention, even though African-American women report intimate partner violence to the police more often—in 66.4 percent of incidents—than other women.

In addition, black women face a greater likelihood of being arrested along with a perpetrator, and their children are more likely to end up in foster care when authorities are involved, Bent-Goodley said in a training webcast last year [2006].

"If I'm being battered, the decision to pick up the phone to call for help is different for me," Lovelace said. "There are more black men incarcerated than there are in college, so that makes it a bigger burden, and I have to question whether he will be brutalized."

Black Female
Victims of Harassment
and Discrimination
Find Little Support

Anne Chapman

Anne Chapman writes for Black Enterprise *magazine.*

Black women who find themselves the victims of harassment and discrimination due to their race, gender, or both, often face a lonely road in trying to right the wrongs that they have endured, Chapman writes in the following article. In some very public cases in the 2000s, the women who are at the heart of the story often feel unsupported, even by those who might normally come to their aid. Women's groups admit that it is difficult to win sexual harassment or gender discrimination cases heard by conservative judges. Chapman goes on to summarize three famous cases, involving Texaco, the New York Knicks, and Supreme Court Justice Clarence Thomas, in which black women struggled to overcome discrimination with mixed results. Nevertheless, most victims contend that overcoming discrimination is a battle worth fighting.

When Don Imus called the Rutgers women's basketball team "nappy-headed hos" and other derogatory names last year [in 2007], there was justified public outcry. In fact, [controversial politician and civil rights advocate] Rev. Al Sharpton led the campaign to get a public apology from the shock jock and advocated for his removal. The end result of the furor: Imus was fired from his popular syndicated CBS Radio show. (He has since returned to the airwaves.)

Anne Chapman, "Race & Gender," *Black Enterprise*, February 2008, pp. 82–88. Reproduced by permission.

Race and Gender Lawsuits

By the end of the summer, another incident involving race and gender was playing out in the tabloids. Former basketball executive Anucha Browne Sanders was in court suing her former boss and employer, New York Knicks President of Basketball Operations and Head Coach Isiah Thomas and Madison Square Garden, for sexual harassment. The story made headline news but there were no protests, outrage, Sharpton—or any other advocacy groups such as the NAACP [National Association for the Advancement of Colored People] or National Organization for Women [NOW]. Browne Sanders fought her battle alone.

Two of the most sensational sexual harassment cases in this country and the largest discrimination suit in history all involved black women: Browne Sanders; Anita Hill, during the 1991 Senate Judiciary hearings on the nomination of Clarence Thomas to the Supreme Court; and Bari-Ellen Roberts, a former senior financial analyst who in 1994 was the lead plaintiff in the discrimination suit against Texaco.

Incidences of sexual harassment and racial discrimination in the private offices and boardrooms of corporate America should be shocking. But even with diversity programs touted as an important business imperative, racism and sexism are still alive and well. And since discrimination can be hard to prove in most cases, those who choose to fight, particularly in the case of black women, often have to go it alone—risking isolation, backlash, and a tarnished reputation.

Women Find Little Support

These women find little support, even from individuals and groups who would be natural advocates. The National Organization for Women has issued a variety of statements against sexual harassment on its Website, even outrage over Imus' return to radio, but it has not listed any coverage or offered any statement of support related to the Browne Sanders case. In her response, NOW President Kim Gandy conceded that women faced tremendous challenges in getting justice on the local and federal levels.

"It's difficult for women, especially women of color, to get a fair shake on these kinds of cases because the courts are heavily stacked with conservatives who are willing to dismiss cases instead of allowing them to be presented to a jury," says Gandy. "But every time a woman prevails in a highly publicized case, it is a victory and gives other women the courage to take a stand and not give up."

Sharpton's usual boisterous protests were also absent from this case, despite media reports showing a taped deposition of Thomas saying it was worse for a white man to call a black woman "a bitch" than for a black man to use such language. Only after Browne Sanders declared victory did Sharpton call for Thomas' apology—not resignation.

Then, in a media flip-flop. Sharpton said he listened to the tape and Thomas' words seemed to have been heavily edited. Suddenly, Sharpton's demand for an apology flew by the wayside. "If he said it," Sharpton argues, "I would have called for him to be fired just like Imus."

Yet Sharpton says he believes the media's negative portrayals of black women force them to prove they deserve respect. "Black women have been miscast as sexual and promiscuous and they have to go to work and live down the videos and stereotypes. Women's rights are a component of civil rights, and we have to do more," says the father of two daughters.

A Lonely Fight

For the women courageous enough to speak out, they understand that their fight will be a lonely one. "When you take a bold step like that, you have to assume that it is your personal step," says Roberts. "It's not wise to think that others will step with you. When I filed my lawsuit, one of the company's attorneys warned me that it would be a long and lonely battle.

She said I would be old and gray, wouldn't have any friends, and she would still be litigating the case—and Texaco would still prosper."

She was wrong: In November 1996, the infamous Texaco "black jelly bean tapes" surfaced and company executives were caught on audio tape planning and plotting to destroy documents that were demanded by the court and by Roberts' attorney. On the tapes, black employees were referred to as "black jelly beans" and called the N-word. The tapes, however, did not surface until two years after Roberts began her suit.

"As a black woman, I had been victimized by discrimination. Every job I went to my race and gender were an issue. I had the education and the experience, but time after time a white man or woman always got the promotion," Roberts explains. "My breaking point and decision to file the lawsuit came because I got tired of Texaco bringing in white boys that I had to train and they would end up with the promotion. It just got to be too much. Winning the case was a huge victory, but I was quick to say the money and the tapes didn't start the suit. The suit was about racism, sexism, and disparity."

The tapes led to the largest settlement in a racial discrimination case. Texaco agreed to pay out more than $176 million to Roberts and other black employees.

Roberts, who detailed her experience in her memoir, *Texaco: A True Story of Race and Corporate America* and is now president of her own management consulting firm, says she cheered when Browne Sanders was awarded $11.6 million in her sexual harassment case against the Knicks, which was later reduced by $100,000.

The Browne Sanders–Isiah Thomas Case

During the trial, Browne Sanders said Thomas sexually harassed her immediately after he became the president for the organization in 2003. She ignored his advances and he became hostile. According to the 18-page lawsuit filed by Browne

Sanders, she was repeatedly called a "bitch" and a "ho" by Thomas. In one interaction, Thomas professed his love for her and suggested they go away and have sex, the lawsuit stated.

At the end of the highly publicized trial, Thomas, 46, denied any wrongdoing and vowed to appeal the verdict. He said the jury got it wrong and he was "extremely disappointed."

Browne Sanders, now the senior associate athletic director at the University of Buffalo, is pleased with the outcome but saddened by what she knows many other women will endure to avoid the scrutiny of associates, colleagues, and the media. "There is a good amount of sexual harassment and discrimination in the workplace: and many women suffer through it in fear of losing their job. The issues I had at Madison Square Garden weren't only happening to me. There were a number of things happening to women who worked for me.

"My breaking point came when they fired me. I wanted to keep my job; I loved my job," she says. "I was in disbelief because I had had years of superior work performance. It was obvious that my firing was retaliation because I complained about the hostile work environment."

It had been estimated that Browne Sanders' payout could have increased significantly for compensatory and punitive damages. But three days before the federal court was to rule, the Garden settled and withdrew all appeals. In punitive damages, the Garden will pay Browne Sanders for creating the hostile work environment and condoning the retaliation against her. Garden Chairman James Dolan will personally have to pay for his retaliatory act of firing her. Thomas was not personally required to pay Browne Sanders.

In the days that followed her victory, two other black women filed discrimination suits against the Garden. Diane Henson and an anonymous co-worker claimed they were denied promotions while young white interns who schmoozed and flirted with managers gained advancement. Henson worked at the Garden for 11 years before she was forced to resign.

Browne Sanders says the problems women face at the Garden are systemic. "When an organization takes a strong stand against discrimination and sexual harassment, that stance will be filtered down."

Dawne Westbrook, Connecticut NAACP legal redress counsel chair and civil rights attorney, says many components come into play after a discrimination lawsuit is filed. "It is often very difficult to file a claim and remain employed," explains Westbrook. "Once the lawsuit is filed, the environment becomes so harassing and hostile that most plaintiffs end up quitting. Then they face the task of trying to find a new job without being blacklisted."

Civil rights attorney Ron Kuby agrees. He says once you file a lawsuit against your current or former employer, it is a big red flag to others that you are "a troublemaker" He maintains: "White male troublemakers are considered movers and shakers, but black women are labeled as people who don't know their place. They are measured by a different scale—no matter how good their work ethic. There is [also] fierce competition for jobs out there, so many black women remain silent."

Westbrook says the NAACP recently became a plaintiff in a discrimination case filed by Cassandra Welch, an 11-year business consultant for Eli Lilly who has now been joined by more than 400 black employees in the class action lawsuit. Welch says she complained about racism, unfair treatment, and pay disparities between white and black employees and immediately became a target of racial harassment.

"Someone put a dark-skinned doll on my desk and tied a noose around her neck. Then the name-calling started and it was sheer shock to me. I couldn't believe it, not in the 21st century. I know racism exists, but it is usually more subtle," she says. "What happened to me was blatant. Prior to speaking up about the unfair treatment, I was a performer and did my job above and beyond what was required. My point was that there should be equal pay and equal merit for equal work. But that is not happening, especially not for black women."

Clarence Thomas and Anita Hill

Ella L.J. Edmonson Bell, associate professor of business administration at the Tuck School of Business at Dartmouth College, says black women in today's workforce feel isolated and alone because they realize early on they are not part of the corporate team and rarely gain the protection of senior executives. "Nobody is out there to look out for black women in the workplace, and that's why they are filing discrimination suits to begin with," says Bell, author of *Our Separate Ways: Black and White Women and the Struggle for Professional Identity*. "I am not surprised when any black woman steps up and files a lawsuit. The problem occurs long before that point. I am surprised more black women are not speaking up."

Brandeis University professor Anita Hill, who declined to be interviewed by BE [*Black Enterprise*] was recently forced to revisit the details of her testimony from 16 years ago [accusing Clarence Thomas of sexual harassment] with the release of Supreme Court Justice Clarence Thomas' memoir, *My Grandfather's Son*. In his book, Thomas says Hill was a liar and her testimony was politically motivated. In a recent *New York Times* Op Ed Hill offered this rebuttal: "I stand by my testimony. Justice Thomas has every right to present himself as he wishes in his new memoir . . . but I will not stand by silently and allow him, in his anger, to reinvent me."

It further stated: "He claims, for instance, that I was a mediocre employee who had a job in the federal government only because he had given it to me. He ignores the reality: I was fully qualified to work in the government, having graduated from Yale Law School and passed the District of Columbia Bar exam, one of the toughest in the nation."

Hill went on to write that Thomas hired her twice, once at the Department of Education and then at the Equal Employment Opportunity Commission. And that she is saddened that Thomas is assassinating her character in order to preserve his.

She stated: "I have repeatedly seen this kind of character attack on women who complain of harassment and discrimination in the workplace. In efforts to assail their accusers' credibility, detractors routinely diminish people's professional contributions. Often the accused is a supervisor, in a position to describe the complaining employee's work as 'mediocre' or the employee as incompetent."

A Price Worth Paying

Browne Sanders, Roberts, and Welch agree that black women pay a hefty price when they decide to speak up about discrimination and sexual harassment in the workplace, but they are confident they did the right thing. "My experience has been frightening," offers Welch, "but I rely on my faith and inner strength. Collectively we have to unite and say we will not tolerate racial and sexual discrimination in the workplace."

White Stereotypes Control African American Women

Maria del Guadalupe Davidson

Maria del Guadalupe Davidson is an assistant professor of African and African American studies at the University of Oklahoma. She is the author of The Rhetoric of Race: Toward a Revolutionary Construction of Black Identity.

In the following viewpoint Davidson states that whites construct stereotypical images of blacks, images that exist primarily in the white imagination, in order to categorize, limit, and control women of color. Four primary images of such women are: the mammy, or black servant to a white family; the matriarch, or the aggressive, unfeminine, bad mother; the breeder, or the welfare mother; and the Jezebel, or sexually wanton and aggressive woman. When the white imagination forces black women into these stereotypes, it constructs an image of a black woman as a problem for whites and reinforces the dominance of white society.

In *Black Feminist Thought*, [sociologist] Patricia Hill Collins's brilliant analysis of "controlling images" explains the status of black women in the white imagination as paradoxically invisible and yet hypervisible at the same time. Black women, placed under "controlling images," become invisible because they are no longer known as individuals but as general types or images. Yet through these very same images, it is also the case that black women become hypervisible. That is to say that "controlling images" render black female existence entirely transparent to white society, thereby making it possible

Maria del Guadalupe Davidson, *Imagining the Black Female Body: Reconciling Image in Print and Visual Culture*. Basingstoke, Hampshire: Palgrave Macmillan, 2010, pp. 194–99. © Carol E. Henderson, 2010. Reproduced with permission of Palgrave Macmillan.

for white men and women to claim full knowledge of the black female experience—an experience that is not their own. Importantly, this type of knowledge does not serve only to construct an image or understanding of black female existence; it also translates into power. In this context [critic] Hortense Spillers has observed, "Let's face it. I am a marked woman, but not everybody knows my name. 'Peaches,' and 'Brown Sugar,' 'Sapphire' and 'Earth Mother,' 'Aunty,' 'Granny,' . . . or 'Black Woman at the Podium.' I describe a locus of confounded identities, a meeting ground of investments and privations in the national treasury of rhetorical wealth. My country needs me, and if I were not here, I would have to be invented." What Spillers, like Collins, adroitly perceives is that black women are a problem that "would have to be invented" by white society. That is to say that such images of black women are necessary to the continued functioning of white society. In order for white society to perceive itself as the norm, then black society must be perceived as deviant from the norm.

As such, "controlling images" become tools to control black women socially, economically, and psychologically. Images of this kind are thus not value neutral; to the contrary, they are constructed by white society in order to perpetuate white dominance and black subservience. In what follows, this insight will be developed through an examination of four dominant controlling images identified by Collins: the Mammy, the Matriarch, the Welfare Mother, and the Jezebel.

The Mammy

The Mammy, with her unusually large breasts and round glowing face, dresses in clothing that signifies work, not play. She is epitomized by actress Hattie McDaniel, who is most often remembered for her portrayal of "Mammy" in *Gone with the Wind*. During most of her career (which ended too soon due to breast cancer), McDaniel went on to play the dramatic role of the black servant to many white families in movies including *In This Our Life* (1942), *The Male Animal* (1942), and *Since You Went Away* (1944). The image of the happy black servant who dutifully cares for her white family more than she does her own, as Phil Patton explains, has a specific social function: "Mammy's legend was created in answer to critics of slavery and Jim Crow; her reality was to become an ambivalent, often haunting register of the complexities of guilt and love white Americans felt. The mythology was created, according to scholars, before the Civil War, as a Southern rebuttal to Northern charges of sexual predation on black women—she was a counterbalance to the octoroon [mixed race] mistress." The icon of the mammy, Patton adds, was created by "white Southerners to redeem the relationship between black women and white men within slave society in response to the antislavery attacks from the North." What is perhaps most interesting here is Patton's claim that the Mammy figure operates as the counterbalance to black women of mixed racial lineage, since Mammy's physical characteristics render her undesirable as a sexual object. In the attempt to desexualize black women, it is clear that the image of both the Mammy and the octoroon are exploited. They play key roles in the larger social narrative constructed by the white imagination, where the octoroon is the object of sexual exploitation and the dark-skinned, sexless Mammy is the servant.

In an effort to understand the normative function of the Mammy image, Collins explains that the Mammy image really exists to justify the economic exploitation of black women in domestic labor. The Mammy who dutifully serves her white family establishes the "normative yardstick used to evaluate all Black women's behavior." In the white imagination, good black women were domestics who loved their "white family" better than their own family, assuming that they had families of their own. As such, the "mammy symbolizes the dominant group's perceptions of the ideal Black female relationship to

Two of the stereotypes that Maria del Guadalupe Davidson says are imposed upon black women are present in this still from the 1929 film Hallelujah, *in which Fanny Belle De-Knight plays Mammy Johnson and Nina Mae McKinney plays the Jezebel-like character Chick.* © John Springer Collection/Corbis.

elite white male power." The image of the black woman at work, while reinforcing the white exploitation of black women's labor, also has a negative impact on the psyche of black women, leading them to internalize their role as servants to white society. Collins argues that black women can internalize this "controlling image" so deeply that they unwittingly transmit it to the black community, and in so doing, "potentially become conduits for perpetuating racial oppression." For Collins, the Mammy image exists in order to show black women that the *safest* way to live in white society is in servitude to white power.

The Matriarch

While the Mammy is enshrined in white imagination as a black female who is compliant to white rule, the Matriarch is the antitype who, according to Collins, "symbolizes the bad Black mother." The Matriarch is typically a single mother who works outside the home in order to support her own family (note that her attention is on the support of her family and not on the white family). She is commonly criticized for not sustaining a traditional home. Thus, her children's inadequate performance in school is a direct result of her lack of "supervision." Collins goes on to describe the Matriarch in the following terms: "As overly aggressive, unfeminine women, Black matriarchs allegedly emasculate their lovers and husbands. These men, understandably, either desert their partners or refuse to marry the mothers of their children." In "Green-eyed Monsters of the Slavocracy: Jealous Mistress in Two Slave Narratives," Minrose C. Gwin helps to extend this point further. For Gwin, it is perplexing that although black women have been traditionally barred from participating in what she calls "The Cult of True Womanhood," black women are still judged by its standards. Black women who assume the primary role as head of household usually are still judged by the false belief that women should be in the home. In such a case, the proverbial cards are "always stacked against" black women. If they stay home their children starve, but if they work they are absent from their children's lives. In both cases, they are accused of being uncaring mothers.

The "controlling image" of the Matriarch, like the Mammy image, is constructed to accomplish a specific social function: to ensure white dominance and the continued subordination of black women. As Collins explains, the image of the Matriarch is used to control black women who do not (or cannot) serve white society. Collins further unmasks the true purpose of the Matriarch image, when she observes that the Matriarch is really a negative stigma applied to women who "dared to violate the image of the submissive, hard-working servant." As a result, it is not surprising that false and imperiling testimonies, such as the [1965] Moynihan Report [which was characterized as blaming the victims of poverty], fail to see the causal impact of white society with regard to negative phenomena plaguing the black community, such as undereducation, high rates of poverty, and the continued ghettoization of black families. The Matriarch image covers over white society's causal role in these negative phenomena and constructs a system of repressive knowledge, where these social failures are attributed to the personal failures of the Matriarch. In this way, Collins goes on to explain, "Those African-Americans who remain poor cause their own victimization. . . . Using images of bad Black mothers to explain Black economic disadvantage links gender ideology to explanations for extreme distributions of wealth that characterize American capitalism."

The Breeder

The third "controlling image" discussed by Collins is that of the "breeder woman" or today's welfare mother. During enslavement, Collins suggests that the controlling image of the breeder woman "portrayed Black women as more suitable for having children than white women." This image places the status of black women on par with livestock and provided justification for "interference in the reproductive rights of enslaved Africans." Enslaved black women were prized for their fertility. "Slave owners wanted enslaved Africans to 'breed,'" Collins writes, "because every slave child born represented a valuable unit of property, another unit of labor, and, if female, the prospects for more slaves." In addition to the link between black female fertility and the institution of slavery, Dorothy Roberts's book *Killing the Black Body* further adds to this account by showing the wrath that infertile black women faced under that institution.

While black fertility was prized during slavery—both as a source of profit and as a means of perpetuating the slavocracy—it came to be demonized afterward, most notably in the "controlling image" of the Welfare Mother. According to Collins, the image of the Welfare Mother is of an overly fertile black woman who is "content to sit around and collect welfare, shunning work and passing on her bad values to her offspring." Without the institution of slavery, white society no longer has a use for this single woman. Consequently, she is now blamed for placing an undue burden on the welfare system. The truth of the matter, however, points in another direction. The American welfare system was introduced in the early twentieth century. Although working black people have contributed to this system since its inception, they were not allowed to collect welfare in any significant way until the 1960s. Since it is clearly a mistake to blame black women for the collapse of the welfare system, Collins rightly observes that "controlling image" of the Welfare Mother really serves to "stigmatize" the black woman as "the cause of her own poverty and that of African-American communities shifts the angle of vision away from structural sources of poverty and blames the victims themselves." In so doing, the Welfare Mother takes the blame for a broken system that she did not create and of which she is not sole beneficiary.

The Jezebel

The final controlling image invoked by Collins is the "Jezebel." The Jezebel is a sexually wanton or "sexually aggressive" woman. Deriving from the time of enslavement, the controlling image of the Jezebel depicts the black woman as hypersexual. This image, like the previous ones, also has a specific social function in white society: it serves to justify the sexual exploitation of black women by white men. Although white men may commit atrocious acts of sexual misconduct, the Jezebel image displaces the cause of their misconduct so that the black woman's hypersexuality takes the blame for the misconduct of white men. Collins goes on to explain that that the Jezebel image reinforces reproductive control over black women. It was believed that since black women are so sexually wanton, they would also be extremely fertile. With this claim, Collins shows that the four "controlling images" of black women described above are all connected in the sense that they construct black female sexuality. Collins observes: "For example, the mammy . . . is a desexed individual . . . typically portrayed as overweight, dark, and with characteristically African features—in brief, as an unsuitable sexual partner for white men. The matriarch represents the sexually aggressive woman. . . . She refuses to be passive and thus is stigmatized. . . . The welfare mother represents a woman of low morals and uncontrollable sexuality. . . . Taken together, these four prevailing interpretations of Black womanhood form the nexus of elite white male interpretations of Black female sexuality and fertility." Ranging from complete desexualization to hypersexualization, these controlling images construct white society's perception of black women and their sexuality. Such images, as we have noted, do not serve primarily to understand the nature of black women, instead they are designed to construct black women as a problem for white society and to reinforce the dominance of white society. These social problems, as we have also noted, are constructed by the white imagination to serve a specific social function, namely, to ensure the continued dominance of white society.

Black Women Equate Hair and Identity

Regina Jere-Malanda

Regina Jere-Malanda is editor of the British magazine New African Woman.

In this viewpoint Jere-Malanda presents an overview of the issues surrounding African American women's hairstyles. The conflict over whether to wear one's hair naturally or use artificial methods of straightening to alter one's look has taken on political ramifications over the years. For women in prominent positions, the choice of how to wear one's hair is seen as an especially important decision, as it influences others. First Lady Michelle Obama is a well-known example of a woman whose style has set a trend. Ultimately, for African American women, one's hairstyle is a reflection of one's identity.

Black women today rarely wear their hair naturally. Next to skin colour, hair is truly the other most visible stereotype of being a black woman. Physically, socially, economically and stylistically, black women's hair is, indeed, not just hair. It is a big deal which evokes serious debate, and here is why:

The Politics of Hair

In the late 1960s, the Afro or natural look became one of the emblems of Black Power, as popularised by the iconic [political activist] Angela Davis. It became a reflection of political and cultural progressiveness, as well as self-esteem, among black people. Fast forward to December 2008, the hairstyle that said "I'm black and proud," has almost disappeared, re-

Regina Jere-Malanda, "Black Women's Politically Correct Hair," *New African Woman*, December 16, 2008, pp. 14–18. Reproduced by permission.

placed by sleek fake-hair weaves and hair extensions or, worse still, hair straightened into submission through chemical creams.

For those of you who may feel a topic of Black women's hair is just another frothy fashion issue, think again. Just try to follow some blogsphere debates in the run-up to the just-ended [in 2008] historic White House race to see just how Michelle Obama's hair took its own political trail.

Check out, for example, the controversial cartoon cover of the *New Yorker* magazine which depicted the Obamas in the Oval Office at the White House, in which Michelle is sporting an Afro and carrying an AK-47. Satire, it was claimed. But to many black people, the message was clear: Afro = angry and militant, reinforcing the age-old prejudice against natural black hair.

But there was even more in cyberspace, as many Black women's blogs dedicated entire forums to debating Michelle's hair. For good reason, in some instances. One in particular— *The Politics of Michelle Obama's hair* by Patricia J Williams— was quite revealing. Although quoted rather at length here for emphasis, her views are, however, just scratching the surface of the hair issue, whose roots run deep, very deep.

"When I graduated from law school in the mid-1970s," says Williams, "African-American women's hair was constantly being scrutinised for signs of subversion: the more 'natural' the more dangerous. So we pressed our hair flat with the weight of other people's expectations and waited for times to change. While curly hair, twists, short Afros, and corn rows are all much more prevalent and tolerated these days, those choices are still publicly interrogated to an unseemly degree. Lani Guinier, Bill Clinton's nominee to head the civil rights division of the Justice Department, was deemed radical in part because of what some commentators called her 'strange hair.' Similarly, when Cynthia McKinney [the Congresswoman who stood as presidential candidate for the little-known Green

Party in the November elections. Yes, there were two black candidates in this election!] changed her hairstyle to corn rows, the [US] Capitol security guards blocked her way, claiming they didn't recognise her as a member of Congress."

Hair and the First Lady

"Most recently," she continues, "in the most-discussed *New Yorker* magazine cover ever, what stood out for me was that Michelle Obama's putative politics were satirised via an Afro! Angela Davis hair! Yes, friends, the hairdo that crossword-puzzle enthusiasts find regularly described as a four-letter synonym for the fashion sensibility of protesters, armed revolutionaries, and frat boys yukking it up in 'fright wigs'. We're talking unequivocally, implacably, no bones about it, political hair. Regardless of how differently the real Davis may wear her hair today, her coif is remembered as a mathematically precise series of explosions, of radioactive microwaves pulsing outward from the sun of the universalised angry black scalp."

Yes, Black women globally couldn't help but notice and discuss Michelle's perfectly coiffed tresses—and in as much as we were moved and inspired by her devotion—filled speeches in support of her husband and country's future—we also wanted to know: who does her hair? What hair products does she use? Is her hair chemically straightened? And so forth. . . .

Acceptable and Unacceptable Fashions

Indeed, while every society in the world has come up with ways, gadgets and products to groom itself for beauty purposes, Black women's hair goes far beyond mere sprucing up and aesthetics. With its history of deep roots in slavery and its politics that change many people's viewpoints, it's a marker of femininity that can influence how the global society embraces the Black woman in both political and social circles. How else can society explain this outrageous scenario at a New York law firm which invited Ashley Baker, then associate editor of the

The controversial July 2008 political cartoon that appeared on the cover of the New Yorker *depicting Michelle Obama wearing an Afro, carrying an AK-47, and giving presidential hopeful husband Barack Obama the Black Power salute.* © Jamie Fine/Reuters/Corbis.

prominent glossy beauty magazine *Glamour,* to speak to them on the "Dos and Don'ts of Corporate Fashion". In a slide show, she says about a Black woman in an Afro hairdo: "A real no-no! As for dreadlocks, how truly dreadful! Shocking that some people still think it's appropriate to wear those hairstyles at the office. No offence, but those political hairstyles really have to go."

Although she resigned soon after, following public outrage and *Glamour* issuing a grovelling apology. Baker touched many raw nerves among Black women, including Afro-wearing Dr Venus Opal Reese, who said in reaction: "When it comes to race, we're looking from the past. When people see me with my natural hair, they don't see Dr Venus Opal Reese who has four degrees, they see an historical idea of what natural hair means. And that's what it meant in the 1970s and 1960s; it equalled Black Nationalism and was linked to the Black Panther Party. It was considered militant. That doesn't mean it's true now, but that's how it's linked." Dr Reese, who is assistant professor of Aesthetics and Cultural Studies at the University of Texas in Dallas, connects hair with culture and politics, whether as an attempt to conform or as a way to declare a revolution. "Some people know wine. I pay attention to hair. I've spent a long time looking at identity formation through hair."

Sad but true, these days the natural Afro look is widely considered unattractive by many Black women (and men), and, as such, not considered fashionable. The past 30 years have seen the Afro replaced by the likes of Jheri curl and dreadlocks in the '80s, braiding, corn rows, locks, and twists in the '90s, and today's rave, the straight-as-a-ruler look—chemically-processed black hair that mimics Caucasian or Asian hair texture and styles—as well as the increasingly popular hair extensions, sown on or glued, to hide the natural look, or the sleek-looking wigs, favoured by women like rapper P Diddy's mother, who is famed for her blonde wigs. To proponents of the natural look, however, chemically straightening Afro hair, or hiding it under fake extensions, is a sign of embracing white superiority over being black, and hence indicates self-hate.

Hair and Identity

But there is even more to Black women's hair in the context of continental Africa. In different countries and communities, hairstyles mean different things. For example, a symbol of woman's marital status, a religious ritual, a mark of ethnicity and geographical origins or even age. In many southern African countries, when a young girl comes of age, her hair is shaven off to symbolise that milestone, and the same ritual is practiced in other areas, when a woman has just been widowed.

As David Coplan, a professor in anthropology at South Africa's Wits University, reckons in *True Love* magazine: "We judge people by appearances and, to an extent, hairstyles signify something about you, so it's natural for people to make assumptions about you based on the way you've styled your hair. Hair and identity are inseparable—whether you're consciously making a statement or not, your hairstyle does express something about you. So if you've been thinking your hair is making no declaration to the world think again."

Yolanda Chapman, who has done extensive research on global attitudes towards Black women's hair-styling practices, believes that Black women have struggled to define themselves in positive terms as both Black and female. "Dealing with issues of beauty—particularly skin colour, facial features, and hair texture—is one concrete example of how controlling images denigrate Black women. Hair, then, is a key site for investigating how Black women's identities are circumscribed by dominant discourses on race and gender. Since Black women have had to learn how to adapt to their sexist and racist environments, one survival strategy they created was 'shifting.'" She explains shifting as a change of outward behaviour, to adopt an alternate pose or voice or embellish a certain identity, in order to satisfy others such as White people or Black men.

She also explains how in the "Black is Beautiful" movement in the 1960s, hair became such a key determinant in visually declaring Black Pride through embracing natural styles, such as the Afro and various braiding styles. After two centuries of slavery, writes Chapman, a self-created system of black hair care was created in the late 1800s with the birth of the black hair-care boom, followed in the early 1900s, by Madam C.J. Walker and Anne Malone, who are famed for creating the massive empire of hair-grooming products targeted at African-American women. Malone wanted, for example, to solve hair problems, such as baldness and breakage, that many Black women of the time faced as a result of a high-stress lifestyle, a nutritionally-deficient diet, and inadequate hygiene. But how things have changed.

A Second Marriage Provides an Opportunity to Do It Right

Pearl Cleage

Pearl Cleage's works include novels, plays, poetry, essays, and performance pieces. Her book What Looks Like Crazy on an Ordinary Day *was a* New York Times *best seller.*

Pearl Cleage reflects on her former relationships, including a boyfriend who abused her and a failed marriage. After divorcing her husband, she enjoyed living on her own and carving out a life in which she did not have to define herself through a man. Even so, a relationship with a close male friend developed into more, and Cleage chose to marry again. This time, she writes, she gave serious thought to getting married. With more life experience behind her, she says, she was able to recognize and appreciate "people who love you not in spite of but because of who you are."

When I met my first husband, I was running for my life. So was he. I was hiding from a former fiancé whose charming attentiveness—which had earned me the admiration of my dorm mates when we started dating—had segued into violent possessiveness. His determination to control my comings and goings culminated in a terrible act: he stripped me naked and tied my hands and feet while he went out one afternoon, admonishing me not to move until he returned, or suffer the consequences. When he did return, he carried me to his bed and forced me to have sex while he whispered a promise to cut my face with razors if I ever left him.

First Husband

My new husband's struggle was less personal, but no less deadly. A strong believer in nonviolence, he was reluctantly interrupting his graduate studies in literature to take a teaching position at a historically Black college. An educational deferment would keep him from joining thousands of other young men on their way to Vietnam. When we met, I had escaped my fiancé's torment by being accepted into a summer program at Yale, which carried a modest stipend. My incredibly ingenious plan to save my life was to forgo my senior year at Howard University, where my lover was anxiously awaiting my return, head for New York City, and, by budgeting carefully, live on my $500 windfall while pursuing my dream of becoming a playwright.

Although I clung to this fantasy throughout the early weeks of the program, I began to sense its inadequacy as the time came to move. My boyfriend's letters, phone calls, and surprise visits to New Haven were evidence that returning to school was not an option if I valued my safety or my sanity, but even I realized that my fantasy of relocating to New York was just that: a fantasy. Other than disappearing into some imaginary Black theater demimonde, the only additional possibility was dragging home in disgrace, so my parents could protect me, a humiliation from which I feared I might never recover.

My trajectory from star student to free woman was in danger of being derailed by a man whose violence I had yet to reveal to friends, family, or fellow students. I was scared and, I realized, unprepared to take care of myself. I had never lived alone, never learned to drive, never balanced a checkbook. From where I was sitting, the world seemed a pretty dangerous place, and although I would have denied it if anybody had asked me directly, what I was looking for was someone to save me. I dreamed of a strong, smart man, making his own way in the world, unintimidated by my boyfriend's rage, convinced that all he needed to make his life complete was a fragile, frightened 20 year old without a clue.

It didn't occur to me until years after our marriage had run its 10-year course that my first husband, in his headlong rush to adjust to the sudden, insistent presence of Uncle Sam, did find exactly what he needed in me: somebody even more terrified of the future than he was. In the face of my helplessness, he felt less vulnerable. He had already successfully lived alone (in New York City, no less), had his own driver's license, and could balance a checkbook without breaking out in a cold sweat. He liked to give directions, and I was trained to take them. After all, I had gotten used to my ex-boyfriend backhanding me across the mouth when I fell short of the mark. My new husband's penchant for stony silences to show his disapproval seemed a small price to pay. I convinced myself we were made for each other.

Divorce

Five years later, the fit that had seemed so perfect in our time of mutual crisis was beginning to chafe. Always a political activist on race and war, I had found a feminist friend and, through her, discovered the women's movement. My violent college love affair no longer seemed shameful evidence of my personal weakness, but part of the larger problem of male violence against women. My frustration at balancing my infant daughter's needs, my husband's demands, and the exhausting requirements of my job as press secretary to Atlanta's first Black mayor was not simply a matter of poor organization, but a problem shared by thousands of women all anxiously searching for new solutions.

Buoyed by the support of my newfound sisterhood, and undeterred by my husband's horrified protests, I left my highly paid, high-profile, high-stress job for a less lucrative parttimer, rented a tiny studio from a colony of artists renovating an old school building, and tried to remember how to write something other than campaign speeches. It was a long, slow, scary, painful process, but as the decade of my 20s came to a close, I had finished a play, found a new apartment, and filed for divorce.

When I signed the papers reclaiming my "maiden" name, I felt a tremendous sense of relief and anticipation. My life was my own for the very first time, and the possibilities seemed endless. I wanted to write and travel and raise my daughter and have my friends over for dinner. I wanted to walk the world's beaches in moonlight, watch the sun rise over the mountains, and learn to ride the New York subways. I wanted to fly the Concorde [supersonic jet liner] to Paris, shave my head, and learn Tai Chi [a Chinese martial art]. I wanted to sip champagne at dawn and drink red wine to stain my lips at midnight. There was no limit to the list of what I wanted to do and only one thing in which I had absolutely no interest: marriage.

In my newly liberated state, the institution seemed hopelessly outdated and relentlessly oppressive. I had had my share of that kind of fun during a decade of domesticity, and although I had every intention of participating fully in what I hoped would be a series of transcendent and transforming love affairs, I would never again define and confine myself by becoming anyone's wife.

That was then. This is now. In March, I will celebrate my second wedding anniversary. Sometimes I look at my husband with such contentment, I can't remember what it was like not having him around, but when I put my mind to it, I can remember absolutely: it was wonderful. At 30, I was a free woman for the first time in my life and loving it. My daughter was growing up sane in spite of my unintentional efforts to drive her crazy. I was figuring out how to make a living as a writer. I was meeting new people who shared my new interests. I was perfecting my lasagna recipe, and watching French movies, so I could approach my newly bohemian life with the proper mixture of joie de vivre [joy of living] and anomie [alienation].

Personal Discovery and Growth

Giddy with the power and pleasure of paying my own way, I was flying solo for the first time in my life. I didn't need a man to fit in socially. My new friends were artists, saxophone players, actors, and activists, straight and gay, young and not so young. Pairing people off boy/girl/boy/girl at sit-down dinner parties was not part of the program. I didn't need a man to support me financially. I was able to pay my bills with a succession of freelance assignments and some part-time teaching jobs. I had found a tiny apartment in a neighborhood that didn't require me to bear arms on routine trips to the grocery store, so I didn't need a man to protect me. And, last, but certainly not least, my biological clock had been beautifully silenced once and for all by the birth of my daughter, by then almost five, so I didn't need a man to help me reproduce. I was free to see men as friends, comrades, lovers, and collaborators who could enrich my life, instead of sustaining it.

It was an exciting time of personal discovery and growth and I had some unforgettable adventures, some interesting near-escapes, and more than my share of tender moments. I even managed to save enough money to buy a house with a real southern magnolia tree out front, some authentic Georgia pines out back, and a side porch where I could sip my tea and watch the world go by. On a balmy summer evening in my new house, I sat laughing and drinking wine with a man who had been my trusted friend and confidant throughout this whole process. I turned to join him in a celebratory toast to the successful completion of one project or another and realized I had, as the [Elvin Bishop] song says, fooled around and fallen in love.

A New Man

My friend was smart, sexy, and single. He made me laugh, and he made me think with the same throwaway charm. He thought my work was important, and I thought his was wonderful. Since we were both writers, we understood the demands of the process and didn't take the craziness personally when the pages wouldn't come, and the deadline was just around the corner. We traded books and walked by the river and struggled over feminist questions that were new to him and still growing in me. We trusted each other to keep the secrets we were whispering in the dark.

I knew I liked him a lot, realized I missed him when we couldn't get together, and looked forward more and more to the times when we could. But love? I didn't want to fall in love. I didn't think I was strong enough to survive it without selling myself out or driving some poor man crazy. On the other hand, I was now old enough to know that the kind of love that this was beginning to feel like was a great gift, not to be taken lightly. After all, I argued with myself, falling in love is fine. Getting married is the problem. Even moving in together (which I realized I was already considering) is not the same as entering into a legal agreement that would subject us to the rules set up by the state of Georgia, the same state whose laws we were already breaking regularly by choosing to have unmarried sex. Besides, both of us had been married once. We had all the children we intended to have, and we did not want or need to involve ministers, state health departments, and official licensing bureaus in the most intimate parts of our lives, again.

Armed with these rationalizations, I welcomed my feelings for my friend, who, it quickly became clear, was way ahead of me. We started spending more and more time together. His presence provided me with something I had missed without ever having had it: another person who saw the world the same way I did, and whose responses to it often mirrored my own.

Gradually, since we were now almost always in each other's presence, we began to talk about living together. Convinced he was completely honorable and would propose no threat to my now adolescent daughter, I waited a few weeks to see if I could talk myself out of it, and when I couldn't, I invited him to move into my house. He accepted with enthusiasm, and we sat down to discuss how to best use the living space to accommodate us.

Since my house had a warm, dry lower level as large as the upper portion, I suggested that we use the house as if it were a duplex, claiming discrete living quarters on our own floors. We would share the washer and dryer (downstairs) and the kitchen (upstairs). Although we anticipated sleeping together most of the time, we each had a bedroom, so our nightly snuggling would continue to be a choice, not a habit or simply a result of having no place else to go. We agreed that if living in close quarters didn't turn out to be as sweet as we hoped, we would go back to separate residences as fast as he could pack the U-Haul.

As it turned out, our arrangement worked even better than we thought it would. The upstairs space continued to be unapologetically gynocentric, accented with sunflowers, the sounds of Sweet Honey in the Rock [an all-women musical ensemble], and photographs of Black women and children, while downstairs was the site of weight lifting and *Monday Night Football* with a sound track by the original Temptations. I enjoyed the increased intimacy without feeling smothered and was delighted to find that everything just seemed to get better.

The Need for Rituals

So the question must be asked, if everything was so good, why mess with success? The answer is simple, and it still surprises me: it was time. I have never been more certain of anything in my life or more called upon to trust my instincts way down at the deepest levels where magic is all that matters. It was time.

The thought first occurred to me one night when we were watching *The Battle of Algiers*, an amazing film that chronicles the bloody struggle for Algerian independence. The French soldiers are relentless in their pursuit of the freedom fighters who are equally tireless in their determination to be free. In the midst of a long siege, filled with betrayal, panic, torture, and death, a young couple seizes a relatively quiet moment for their long-delayed wedding ceremony.

Surrounded by the rubble of bombed-out buildings and the burned shells of ruined automobiles, the young bride drapes a wedding veil over her head and clasps the hand of her lover, who joins his vows with hers against a background of approaching gunfire. Their passionate embrace at the end of the brief ceremony seems the only antidote to the murder and madness. Their fierce determination to proclaim and celebrate their love seems an act of such power and purity that it alone is capable of ensuring their own survival, the survival of their beleaguered band, and, by extension, the Algerian people.

As an African American woman whose community, beset by AIDS, crack, unemployment confusion, and self-hate, is in perhaps the worst shape since slavery, I identified strongly with the need for rituals to strengthen and renew us collectively. I was drawn to the faith that the simple ceremony exemplified. Watching the couple promise each other their lives, something in me felt that it was time for me to make some vows of my own. I felt an emotional shift, a glimmer of understanding of the fact that because I was new, any marriage I entered could also be new. Our acceptance of the roles we played as conscious Black artists was now clearly the foundation of a love that not only sustained and nurtured the two of us but also connected us to a wider struggle to sustain and nurture the group of which we were a part.

So Far, So Good

That was the first time I thought seriously about getting married. The second time is harder to describe, having mainly to do with revelations reached at 35,000 feet, which are always suspect because of the effects of airplane air and a vodka and tonic before boarding. Suffice it to say, on a flight home from a trip that I couldn't wait to finish, I absolutely knew, with a perfect peace, that I wanted to marry and share my life as fully and as honestly and passionately as I knew how. I wanted to say yes, up front and out loud, when we were being pushed on every side to say no, to live no, to be no. I wanted to make the effort as my mother and grandmothers and their grandmothers had; the effort to find love among what were supposed to be ruins. I was sure. It was time.

When he finally agreed, after waiting overnight to be sure I was sure and not just glad the plane had landed safely, we got a license and paid our fee and called our friends and lit the candles and asked the judge if he could do it at our house, and he said yes. And Joe played the saxophone, and my daughter stood up with me, and the best man smiled over my husband's shoulder when he heard me say, "I do." Afterward, we drank champagne and hugged each other as tightly as we could. We're old enough this time around to know how rare it is to share a perfect moment with people who love you not in spite of but because of who you are. So far, so good.

For Further Discussion

1. What factors in Hurston's life made her a complex figure who had many friends as well as enemies? Why did she fall out of favor with the literary establishment? (See Lowe, Headon, and Wall.)

2. Is *Their Eyes Were Watching God* a feminist book or does Janie's story conflict with the core beliefs of feminism? (See Harris.)

3. Does Janie truly find love and happiness with Tea Cake, or is this episode just a romantic fantasy that cannot last? (See Rosenblatt and Smith.)

4. Do you view the ending of *Their Eyes Were Watching God* as triumphant and happy or defeatist and sad? What is the likelihood that Janie will die of rabies? (See Rosenblatt, Smith, and Hattenhauer.)

5. African American women have long been the victims of stereotyping. How are contemporary African American women fighting these ingrained notions and carving out their own independent lifestyles? (See Chapman, Davidson, and Cleage.)

For Further Reading

Maya Angelou, *I Know Why the Caged Bird Sings*, 1969.

Ralph Ellison, *Invisible Man*, 1952.

Lorraine Hansberry, *A Raisin in the Sun*, 1959.

Zora Neale Hurston, *Dust Tracks on a Road*, 1942.

Zora Neale Hurston, *Jonah's Gourd Vine*, 1934.

Zora Neale Hurston, *Moses, Man of the Mountain*, 1939.

Zora Neale Hurston, *Seraph on the Suwanee*, 1948.

Terry McMillan, *Waiting to Exhale*, 1992.

Toni Morrison, *Beloved*, 1987.

Toni Morrison, *The Bluest Eye*, 1970.

Gloria Naylor, *The Women of Brewster Place*, 1982.

Ntozake Shange, *For Colored Girls Who Have Considered Suicide, When the Rainbow Is Enuf*, 1975.

Alice Walker, *The Color Purple*, 1982.

Richard Wright, *Native Son*, 1940.

Bibliography

Books

Michael Awkward   *New Essays on "Their Eyes Were Watching God"*. Cambridge: Cambridge University Press, 1990.

Harold Bloom   *Zora Neale Hurston*. New York: Chelsea House, 1986.

Valerie Boyd   *Wrapped in Rainbows: The Life of Zora Neale Hurston*. New York: Scribner, 2003.

Gloria L. Cronin   *Critical Essays on Zora Neale Hurston*. New York: G.K. Hall, 1998.

Henry Louis Gates and Anthony Appiah   *Zora Neale Hurston: Critical Perspectives Past and Present*. New York: Amistad, 1993.

Robert E. Hemenway   *Zora Neale Hurston: A Literary Biography*. Urbana: University of Illinois Press, 1980.

Karla F.C. Holloway   *Alice Walker and Zora Neale Hurston: The Common Bond*. Westport, CT: Greenwood Press, 1993.

Lucy Anne Hurston   *Speak, So You Can Speak Again: The Life of Zora Neale Hurston*. New York: Doubleday, 2004.

Zora Neale Hurston and Carla Kaplan   *Zora Neale Hurston: A Life in Letters*. New York: Doubleday, 2002.

| Lovalerie King | *The Cambridge Introduction to Zora Neale Hurston*. Cambridge: Cambridge University Press, 2008. |

Susan Edwards Meisenhelder — *Hitting a Straight Lick with a Crooked Stick: Race and Gender in the Work of Zora Neale Hurston*. Tuscaloosa: University of Alabama Press, 1999.

Diana Miles — *Women, Violence and Testimony in the Works of Zora Neale Hurston*. New York: Peter Lang, 2002.

Deborah G. Plant — *Every Tub Must Sit on Its Own Bottom: The Philosophy and Politics of Zora Neale Hurston*. Urbana: University of Illinois Press, 1995.

Deborah G. Plant — *Zora Neale Hurston: A Biography of the Spirit*. Westport, CT: Praeger, 2007.

Alice Walker — *Anything We Love Can Be Saved*. New York: Ballantine Books, 1998.

Cheryl A. Wall — *Zora Neale Hurston's "Their Eyes Were Watching God": A Casebook*. Oxford: Oxford University Press, 2000.

Periodicals

Bertram D. Ashe — "Why Don't He Like My Hair?: Constructing African-American Standards of Beauty in Toni Morrison's *Song of Solomon* and Zora Neale Hurston's *Their Eyes Were Watching God,*" *African American Review*, Winter 1995.

Claire Crabtree "The Confluence of Folklore, Feminism and Black Self-Determination in Zora Neale Hurston's *Their Eyes Were Watching God*," *Southern Literary Journal*, Spring 1985.

Angela P. Dodson "Exposing Triple Myths: Dr. Melissa V. Harris-Perry Explores the Black Woman's Challenge to Move Beyond Race, Gender Stereotypes and to Be Recognized as an Authentic Individual," *Diverse Issues in Higher Education*, September 1, 2011.

Economist "Down or Out; Unmarried Black Women," October 15, 2011.

SallyAnn Ferguson "Folkloric Men and Female Growth in *Their Eyes Were Watching God*," *Black American Literature Forum*, Spring–Summer 1987.

Jennifer Jordan "Feminist Fantasies: Zora Neale Hurston's *Their Eyes Were Watching God*," *Tulsa Studies in Women's Literature*, Spring 1988.

Missy Dehn Kubitschek "Tuh De Horizon and Back: The Female Quest in *Their Eyes Were Watching God*," *Black American Literature Forum*, Autumn 1983.

Donald R. Marks "Sex, Violence, and Organic Consciousness in Zora Neale Hurston's *Their Eyes Were Watching God*," *Black American Literature Forum*, Winter 1985.

Shawn E. Miller   "'Some Other Way to Try': From Defiance to Creative Submission in *Their Eyes Were Watching God*," *Southern Literary Journal*, vol. 37, no. 1, 2005.

Julie Roemer   "Celebrating the Black Female Self: Zora Neale Hurston's American Classic (Reclaiming the Canon)," *English Journal*, vol. 78, no. 7, 1989.

Joseph R. Urgo   "The Tune Is the Unity of the Thing: Power and Vulnerability in Zora Neale Hurston's *Their Eyes Were Watching God*," *Southern Literary Journal*, Spring 1991.

Alice Walker   "In Search of Zora Neale Hurston," *Ms.*, March 1975.

S. Jay Walker   "Zora Neale Hurston's *Their Eyes Were Watching God*: Black Novel of Sexism," *Modern Fiction Studies*, vol. 20, 1975.

Index